D1505316

HUGOLIAD

or

THE GROTESQUE AND TRAGIC LIFE
OF VICTOR HUGO

by
EUGÈNE IONESCO

postscript by
GELU IONESCU

translated from the Romanian into French by
DRAGOMIR COSTINEANU
with the participation of
MARIE-FRANCE IONESCO
translated from the French by
YARA MILOS

GROVE PRESS
NEW YORK

Copyright © 1982 by Editions Gallimard

English language translation Copyright © 1986 by Yara Milos

Originally published in French in 1982 under the title Hugoliade by Editions Gallimard, Paris

All rights reserved.

No part of this book may be reproduced, stored in a retrieval system, or transmitted in any form, by any means, including mechanical, electronic, photocopying, recording or otherwise, without prior written permission of the publisher.

First Grove Press edition 1987
First printing 1987
ISBN: 0-394-54139-1
Library of Congress Catalog Card Number: 84-48460

Library of Congress Cataloging-in-Publication Data

Ionesco, Eugène.
   Hugoliad : or the grotesque and tragic life of Victor Hugo.

   1. Hugo, Victor, 1802-1885 — Biography — Anecdotes,
facetiae, satire, etc.   2. Authors, French — 19th
century — Biography — Anecdotes, facetiae, satire, etc.
I. Title.
PQ2293.I57   1986   848'.709   [B]   84-48460
ISBN 0-394-54139-1

Designed by Abe Lerner

GROVE PRESS, INC., 920 Broadway
New York, N.Y. 10010

5   4   3   2   1

Contents

Preface

I was quite young when I wrote this text on Victor
Hugo. Then I completely lost sight of it. It was dis-
covered in an old Romanian review.

I thank Mr. Costineanu for his research and translation, and my daughter Marie-France, who was
good enough to help us and check the French text.

In my youth I was very fond of debunking (de-
mystifying, one would say nowadays) great men, in-
stitutions (what some years ago was known as the
establishment). Well, Victor Hugo seemed to me at
the time both a great man and an institution. The
ironic biography I wanted to write was not finished.
It stops at the forty-sixth year, I think, of the great
genius. Before the advent of the Second Empire.
When I wrote this book decades ago, eloquence was
out of style and Verlaine's precept was observed:
"Take eloquence and wring its neck." With Victor
Hugo it was the eloquence that bothered me. Those
were also the days when André Gide would answer,
if asked who was the greatest French poet: "Victor
Hugo, alas." And Cocteau said: "Victor Hugo was a
madman who thought he was Victor Hugo." To write
this study, I remember now, was hard work. I had

read some nineteenth-century criticism, especially three or four books on the life of Victor Hugo, completely forgotten today, by E. Biré, his fierce detractor.

I wanted above all to amuse myself, to scandalize. Already I distrusted literature and men of letters.

Politics did not interest me yet. I had no political objectives in this little work. It was an exercise in mischief, a work of youth.

EUGÈNE IONESCO

May 1982

Foreword

Hugoliade, ou La Vie grotesque et tragique de Victor Hugo
("The Grotesque and Tragic Life of Victor Hugo"), a
work of Eugène Ionesco's youth, rediscovered thanks
to miraculous circumstances and the assistance and
goodwill of several "Ionescans" (to whom we express
our appreciation), reprinted here as initially published in "preview" form in a Romanian journal of the
1930s, untraceable in any library large or small in the
Western world, is finally published in book form for
the first time.

The twenty-six-year-old author presents us with
the funniest and most grotesque episodes of the first
forty-four years in the life of the great French romantic poet, his amorous tribulations and his histrionics
(facts and events supported by authentic docu-
ments).

Victor Hugo, the patriarch of French poetry, in
drawers (longjohns, if you please!), seedy, come
down from his plumed and gaudy throne, a god de-
mythologized, a bluffer unmasked, a kitsch Victor
Hugo (too bad this word, which would have made a
perfect title for this work, did not exist in the
1930s) — that is what Ionesco offers us. In a way, it is

a double revelation. On the one hand, a "national" poet presented from his "best" angle — on the other, a young Romanian critic "trying his hand" at literature. Above all, a revelation for the French public, which already knew Ionesco as playwright, short-story writer, novelist and literary or political columnist, unlike the prewar Romanian public, which knew him as literary critic (young nonconformist critic) and poet.

Actually, apart from the fact that it is a passionate text, bizarrely passionate and passionately bizarre, *Hugoliad* is a text that is supremely unclassifiable in any of the known literary genres and at the same time classifiable in all and each — or almost so: poetry, literary criticism, (anti-)biography and novel. Or, as Gelu Ionescu said: "His work is at once a lampoon, a parody and a polemic."

In short, it is a text of literary virtuosity and artistic bravura. And we must not forget that it is an unfinished writing! In keeping with the necessary sense of mystery, it is not known whether the ending has been lost or was never written (it has not, in any event, been published) — and that (supreme quality!) does not matter at all in this text, a "concentrate" of all Eugène Ionesco's art.

It is a kind of antihagiographic and satirical "monograph" on Hugo the *"monstre sacré,"* full of humor and irony.

It is a funny work. It is a sad work.

DRAGOMIR COSTINEANU

i

PRESENTATION, *or rather*
APHORISMS

*"Une belle âme et un beau talent poétique sont
presque toujours inséparables."[1]* — Victor Hugo

VICTOR HUGO'S father, General Count Léopold-
Sigisbert Hugo, was a sort of rough and simple
trooper, sufficiently devoid of scruples to abandon
his wife and very young children. Infatuated with a
bogus Spanish countess, he went and set himself up
in Spain, where he governed a province in the name
of Napoleon I. Victor Hugo's mother, Sophie, who
for that matter was not an ideal spouse, left for Spain
with her children but failed to reconquer the count
for all that. Too proud to bear being replaced by
another woman, she bolted back to Paris with the
children and in turn replaced her husband with General Lahorie: an eye for an eye, a tooth for a tooth.

Léopold-Sigisbert Hugo, son of a carpenter, was
ennobled by Napoleon. Yet his name was not en-
graved on the Arc de Triomphe — a fact that infuri-
ated him beyond measure and also outraged Victor
Hugo later on. No doubt he considered himself un-
justly used. He must have thought his title, like the

governance of a province, too small a reward for his great services and doughty deeds. This count and colonel of Napoleon's received, as a belated and indirect reward, the rank of general under the Bourbon Restoration.

If Léopold-Sigisbert Hugo was impulsive and dominated by a crude sensuality, he nevertheless had a sort of flair we might call literary, though totally lacking in taste and discretion, a flair inherited and amplified by Victor Hugo to proportions we well know. In the name of this literature, Léopold-Sigisbert Hugo once confided to Victor Hugo in the strictest intimacy:

"You were conceived *sur un des pics les plus elevés des Vosges*," and he specified: "*lors d'un voyage de Lunéville à Besançon.*"[2]

Sophie too was proud, but her pride was in better taste. She loved General Lahorie, and above all she admired him, which irritated Léopold-Sigisbert to the limit. This General Lahorie, adventurer and anti-Bonapartist conspirator, is undoubtedly the strangest and most interesting man in this whole story about Hugo. I admit that I would have preferred to concern myself with him instead of the great romantic poet. That's not what Sophie Hugo thought. In the final analysis, her affair with Lahorie did not have very important consequences, for she didn't neglect Victor because of it — and she is the main culprit of his career. She made him renounce the Polytechnic, a course of study as suited to his immense capacity for work as to his limited intelligence, and threw him into literature.[3] At the time literature and poetry prevailed over the conduct of affairs of state, for nations then allowed poets to lead them. Nowadays it would be absolutely ridiculous to try to satisfy one's pride by being a poet. The inflation of poetry has necessarily led to its depreciation. And today it has again become what it should always have remained: a Cinderella. But because this was an epoch of soldiers and poets — rather of poets since the fall of Napoleon — Sophie imposed poetry upon Victor. Not that it was difficult for her; young Victor's temperament was excellent terrain on which her own ambitions could thrive. So deep were the roots of Sophie's vanity that she easily overcame both her poor health and her fear of death. Thus it happened that the adolescent Victor was once sitting up with her during a grave illness. Victor Hugo stayed all the while at his sick mother's bedside and no longer had time to write poems. Sophie, pale, turned her head toward him and made an effort to speak:

"*L'o . . .*" she said in a faint voice.

"*De l'eau?*" Victor asked, thinking she wanted water.

"No. *L'o-de!*"

"The ode?"

"Yes. The ode[4] that you are to submit for the prize of the Toulouse Academy! Have you written it?"

"No."

"Write it here, now," she said to him in her faint voice.

And Victor, submissive, wrote at the bedside of this Hugolian character lines that had nothing to do with the reality of the moment:

Je voyais s'élever dans le lointain des âges,
Ces monuments, espoir de cent rois glorieux . . .[5]

And the ode on *Le Rétablissement de la statue de Henri IV* ("The Restoration of the Statue of Henry IV") restored Sophie, who on this occasion stopped dying.[6]

Thus will Victor Hugo proceed later on, for the rest of his life: poems, literature, eloquence along the periphery of great grief, independent of the grief and of the major events in life. From then on he enrolls himself in the school of vanity and insensitivity. He will systematically lose every chance of living serious experiences — henceforth his sufferings will be false and literary. He will never be his own master. He will be condemned to insensitivity and superficiality, to vanity, to the venal love of glory and applause that will suborn his spiritual values.

By imbuing her son with even more vanity instead of striving to curb this trait, by exaggerating the parvenu's mentality that he had in any case inherited from Léopold-Sigisbert, by handing down to him her own unbounded ambitions, Sophie Hugo assured Victor's literary glory. In effect, to become a great man, one need only will it passionately. Learn the famous man's trade as one learns the carpenter's trade. It is characteristic of the biography of the famous man that he wanted to be famous. It is characteristic of the biography of Everyman that he did not want to be, or did not think of being, a famous man. All that is required to succeed is a strong desire to succeed; one must be dominated by an absurd, ridiculous and total passion for outward appearances, the inessential, the insubstantial. The philosopher who serves ideas, the politician who serves the state, the writer who serves literature, they all wanted first of all to serve themselves. It is not a logical, political or artistic problem that interests them — but fame, their first and most important impulse. It is true that the idea, that scamp, acts by itself and that while getting what's in it for them, great men unwittingly let slip through their fingers that which becomes part of the history of culture. In fact, genius is but the protracted will to be a genius. The protracted, indefatigable and relentless will. A will without reversals, without re-grets, without the sentiment of uselessness: a con-fused uselessness, unaware of being useless. The man of fame and genius is the man who gives up every-thing truly essential, all aspirations, all the spirit's absolutes. A famous man is a false devotee and a disgusting arriviste. The man of genius or great talent is an abdicator of the spirit, a failure, a muddlehead, a monomaniac obsessed with himself, the quintessence of all vanities — whereas the Saint's only obsession is God. The genius loves himself more than he should. His own absorbing vanities are opinionated and closed. His selfishness is immense and obstinate. His thirst for success makes him master highly esteemed social values: zest, talent, polemical force, etc., things that anyone with a little tenacity can master. Genius is social and therefore never disinterested, never gra-tuitous. No famous man is brilliant or famous without knowing it and having wanted to be so. All glory is the prize of a spiritual deficiency. A rape of the soul of things. One achieves nothing by the fact that one loves, but by the fact that one loves or hates what one is not. And for their own self-fulfillment the various Victor Hugos cultivate talent as they would real estate, tend it very carefully, maintain it as an inheritance that must be expanded at all costs, improve it and risk it in diverse speculations, as on the stock exchange. For talent is molded, cultivated — predispositions are inherited. One can also build talent by a kind of specialization, by exercises similar to sports that develop a certain part of the body — the legs, the arm muscles, the chest, etc. — to the detriment of the rest. Talent is specialization, education through exercise and the training of certain general qualities. The average man can become as talented *as he wants to* (if he knows how to want) and even, at a given moment, brilliant. To be talented is no more honorable than to be rich. But the higher one rises spiritually, the poorer one becomes. The Saint has neither genius nor talent.

To be truthful, a great talent like Victor Hugo's has exactly the same meaning from an intellectual point of view as a tenor's voice. The opinion of such men as Veuillot, Leconte de Lisle, Ernest Renan, A. France, etc., who said that Victor Hugo was a genius and a simpleton, seems to me highly significant. These things are not paradoxical but extremely obvious. I sincerely believe that a far less than mediocre intelligence cannot prevent the blossoming of genius. But if a tenor knows that all he has is a good voice and that his voice is just a voice, Victor Hugo has the right (accorded by whom, I don't know) to pretend that his tenor's voice also ordains him philosopher, states- man, reformer and prophet. For that matter, there was a time when certain men like Lamartine and Victor Hugo were pushed into the foreground be- cause it was believed that tenors were *it,* and that it was necessary to be guided in political life, cultural life and spiritual life by tenors and nothing but ten- ors. But this is still believed today, as it will always be believed. Victor Hugo had the great fortune, in his spiritual life, of having talent and becoming rich too. In the face of these virtues Théophile Gautier, by his own admission, fainted with emotion at the sight of Hugo and the host of people groveling at his feet. Instead of curing the vain of their vanity, men en- courage them by swooning. Among the imbeciles whom Victor Hugo bowled over, one should mention Brunetière, if only because his foolishness was chronic: Notably, he stated that "Hugo's verses are pleasant even on rereading"—whereas the only rea- son for the survival of Victor Hugo's work is that it can't be read even once. But it is the fault of a vulgar education that admiration for Victor Hugo goes to such lengths as: *"Elevés dans l'amour de la gloire et de la génie, pour nous V. Hugo était un nom presque aussi mer- veilleux que Homère ou Virgile."*[7] The kowtowing and prostration were such that it could be said of the poet:

"Et je lui disais Maître, humblement, tendrement"[8] — surprising words today, of course, even when the fawning dog calls himself Fernand Gregh.

If Victor Hugo's talent is composed of his spiritual deficiencies, it is clear that this talent is itself deficient.

"Victor Hugo was not a poet but an orator," as Rémy de Gourmont was the first to say, if I am not mistaken, and as was repeated afterwards by so many others. This holds universally with the evident force of an axiom, while an equitable judgment (Brunetière's, though he didn't know what he was saying) shows that the considerable influence of Victor Hugo was not due to his ideas, which were rather paltry, but to the metaphorization of his paltry ideas, and thus projects this poet completely outside the realm of poetry. It so happens that from a certain remove, not of time but of altitude, one loses the meaning of a historico-literary appraisal when one ceases to regard values in a necessarily chronological order and takes a synoptic view: This is one reason why Victor Hugo may now be regarded clearly, freely, as he was, this is why we do not like him today. In fact, in judging a value from the viewpoint of the necessity of the historical moment, one judges the historical moment, how the value is determined, and not the value itself. Fifty years later, the different "values" imposed by historical or historico-literary moments are filtered, subject to the test of more disinterested, freer criteria. One cannot say definitively that these criteria are absolute either, but they are firmer because they are, or can be, independent. In effect, there is a psychology of the historical moment, identical to mass psychology, in which suggestion plays the most effective role. Nothing can be thought; everything is imposed.

He is heard who cries the loudest, who talks the most, who represents the collective mentality of the moment, irrespective of any spiritual attitude. Later on, farther away, the cries and exigencies fade, no longer impress, and the man can be judged — falsely, to be sure, because all human judgments are false — but more subtly and more lucidly. Thus is it established that Victor Hugo's talent is of the same poor quality as Arghezi's:[9] verbose, elementary, instinctive. If Victor Hugo was a good maker of metaphors, it is precisely because he had a limited mind and because his vision was sensory, physical, plastic. The dictionary of Hugo's metaphors assembled by Duval shows us which were the poet's preferred images: the eye, the star, the flower, the earthworm, the flame, the shadow, the snake, the hydra — visual obsessions. Victor Hugo did not know that the metaphor could be one of poetry's conditions but not poetry itself. He did not know that eloquence accompanied by metaphors is the negation of poetry. Victor Hugo is eloquent and rich in metaphors as is a torrent. I don't see why men are so fond of torrents in poetry and intellectual life and do not equally appreciate in poetry, for example, the life force of buffalos. Victor Hugo's torrent is in fact only a spilt bucket, straw and dirty water. Romanticism had an exaggerated love of straw and dirty water. Victor Hugo was so well loved because it was believed that poetry is a dictionary, a dictionary of words or metaphors; it was believed that poetry can be rhetoric and noise — and the belief was so great that Victor Hugo poeticized and spoke of silence with noise, of death with eloquence, of nothingness with plastic images. This presses like a weight on my heart and — there it is — I feel I'll never be able to forgive Victor Hugo for it. However, the bankruptcy of Hugo clearly proves that poetry is neither vocabulary nor historical grammar nor philology nor linguistics. Poetry is not lexical expression but a mode of expression. It is emotion given, not theorized. It is outcry, not discourse. It isn't even the development of an exclamation, as Valéry says, but the exclamation itself. Poetry partakes of the spirit's purest and most fundamental life. There exists for poetry a biology of the spirit, independent of intellectual as well as physical life, which the Hugolian vision, for example, sullies. Poetry frees itself from logic and discourse, while images are but the steps it must climb and surpass, steps on which it must only rest its foot. Poetry's primitiveness is transcendental. It is a spiritualized biology. An effort to reach beyond matter to the summits of the spirit. That is why it is a moan, a cry (poetry wrenches itself free of matter, lets it go, separates from it), that is why it cleanses itself of colors, images, noises, after colors were its first stage of purification.

One must not confuse a poet with a man of talent. A man of talent is a social man. A poet is not talented because he is not social and because talent is manual dexterity, which the poet disdains. The fate of true poets is never to be successful. The heavy, gross images of Victor Hugo's poetry indicate a primitive-sensual vision of the world — while poetry has only a spiritual primitiveness.

Perhaps the young Victor Hugo, author of *Odes et*

ballades ("Odes and Ballads") and later *Les Orientales*
("Oriental Poems"), was a promising poet between
the ages of twenty and twenty-seven. He needed to
concentrate himself, to become authentic, to plumb
his own depths. He completely bungled his poetic
destiny. Everything that was still a pure vibration of
the heartstrings was replaced by heavy ham-
merblows. He dealt the final blow to emotion by undertaking a literary apprenticeship with an eye to
minting it. He could no longer express any emotion,
any cry, any lament. He could manage no more than
to speculate thereupon. Thus, instead of concentrating himself, he diluted himself and acquired an external cleverness that made him glib; instead of learning
to keep silent, henceforth he could only talk.

And all this because he was ambitious. If despite
all his intellectual deficiencies and his materialistic
vision of the world a penetration toward the sources
of his inner self could have saved him as a poet, his
vanity, his lyrical speculation and his eloquence decreed that this poet — this potential poet — became a
man of letters: a famous man of letters, a glorious
man of letters, duly ridiculed nowadays, when Victor
Hugo can only constitute material for philologists,
grammarians and linguists, but not poetry for poets.
Prosper Mérimée, austere Mérimée who always
knew how to check verbal dissolution and debauchery, was right when he wrote in *Lettre à une inconnue*
("Letter to an Unknown Woman, 1862) that Hugo is
a man *"qui se grise de ses paroles et qui ne prend pas la
peine de penser."*[10] It is quite true that Victor Hugo
never took the trouble to think. He really didn't have

time. He was too busy to be able to think of either his life or his death. Besides, to become a great man, it is never necessary to think of these things. These things only prevent you from advancing or make you fall behind. The future great man hurls himself into life with eyes that look only outward, never inward. The ambition of the future great man should be so overwhelming that it leaves room for nothing else: neither thought nor love nor suffering — unless it is the suffering of vanity. The future great man must swim forever in pure, guileless, unabridged vanity, without remorse, without introspection. He must have time to think about death. To believe that one does not die.

Victor Hugo had glory, assets, power. He had everything. But his assets were frittered away time and again; his power was intermittent; and today his glory is shaken from top to bottom. He has nothing left. But this is what always happens to great men, to the Don Quixotes and the Tartarins: In the end they have nothing left.

Victor Hugo was a typical great man. He did not know how to exist for himself or for the world; yet he believed he belonged to himself, and the world believed he belonged to the world. The essential condition of glory: He knew how to be and not be for everyone, which is to say, representative. He was, fittingly, a man of exemplary mediocrity. He was banal, common and obedient to the crowd, which led him by the nose. He belonged perfectly to the historical moment, this slave of all the historical moments of his life.

A famous man, a talent, is imposing to the extent

he allows himself to be imposed upon, to the extent he obeys. Historical laws impose him on the world. He follows historical laws. He is their slave. A classical vision, for example, could not have flourished in 1830: It would have drowned in the waters of romanticism.

Victor Hugo, after having hesitated for some time during his adolescence and early youth, learned how to be what he was asked to be. And his instinct never deceived him afterwards. If his talent had to overcome obstacles, that hardly means it was any the less exciting for him. And as for his celebrated prefaces, they were officially revolutionary since the revolutionary regime was in power. Victor Hugo knew perfectly well with whom to travel. And since the crowd can only bring forth geniuses who belong to it and symbolize emptiness for it, Victor Hugo, poor fellow, might be taken for a magician, a superman, a poet of the stature of Dante or Virgil.

The truth is that a lofty spirituality never makes the mistake of allying itself with genius or talent. It does follow the call of the masses but only allows itself to be influenced by those from a higher realm. It vanquishes, it repels the call of the masses, or else frees itself from them.

Nevertheless, *"Une belle âme et un beau talent poétique sont presque toujours inséparables,"* Victor Hugo stated in one of his notorious *Lettres à la fiancée* ("Letters to a Fiancée"), with his characteristic lack of lucidity.

In what follows we shall see time and again how "a beautiful soul" allies itself inseparably with "a great talent." . . .

Vanity, his ruling passion, urged Victor Hugo to aspire to be a great political figure. Although matters are not yet too serious, his vanity has obscured even his personal affections by falsifying and reducing them to superficiality, and has completely annulled his spiritual life.

He did not set out to write poems just to write poems but simply because from the age of fourteen he wanted to be "Chateaubriand or nothing."[11] Later he came to regard Chateaubriand as unbearably distant and proud. His dislike turns into admiration the day Chateaubriand receives him in his nightshirt and proceeds to brush his teeth in front him. This intimacy so enchants him that, filled with enthusiasm and gratitude, he goes straight home and composes the ode to *Le Génie* ("The Genius").[12] He does everything possible to assure his literary glory and publicize himself, confessing at the same time in a letter to a friend that "applause sweetens my success."[13] He deceives his publishers and, using Célestin Nanteuil as a screen, secures an audience for himself at performances of his plays and at the frequent public hearings of his lawsuits before the courts. Nicknamed "Grand Master of Publicity," he commissioned Sainte-Beuve to sing his praises.

Victor Hugo made Victor Hugo come true thanks to vanity, envy, jealousy and all kinds of petty motives too shameful to be confessed. It is nonetheless true that such pettiness is creative. Furious at the unseemly success of his good friend Dumas *père* with the play *Henri III et ∂a cour* ("Henry III and His Court"), performed in February 1829, Hugo attacks him, signing his criticism with the initials of a straw man. Pale, livid with envy, he is not satisfied until he himself writes a number of plays — with which you are familiar — whose success, though challenged, he had staged beforehand. He withdraws from the 1824 and 1829 literary *cénacles* because in the company of Vigny, Charles Nodier, Sainte-Beuve, Lamartine, Dumas *père,* Delacroix and Musset, he could not monopolize the limelight, and he founds his own literary *cénacle* in 1836, composed of such mediocrities as Bouchardy, Célestin Nanteuil, Auguste Mac Keat and Petrus Borel, who were forever attending his theatrical productions and plotting on his behalf. He pursues his critics with mortal hatred and even dismisses Désiré Nisard from the *Journal des Débats* ("Journal of Debate") although he was penniless and recently married, merely because the man had certain reservations — all the while writing *Arbres vous connaissez mon âme* ("Trees, You Know My Soul") and many other poems filled with fine sentiments.

Furthermore, as long as he lived and as much as he wrote on forgiveness, goodness and the fine sentiments, he never forgot his critics (Nisard, Mérimée, Montalembert), and he insulted them in his memoirs, in his prose, in his verse, at every opportunity, styling them boors, scoundrels, riffraff, pests, etc.

His wife, Adèle, he neglects completely, using her only to arrange his theatrical successes. Absorbed as he was in his literary glory and Juliette Drouet, he refuses to notice that Sainte-Beuve is falling in love with Adèle. He refuses to notice even when Sainte-Beuve intimates it to him. He contents himself with moral blackmail, demanding publicity and articles on his books. When Sainte-Beuve openly admits that he loves Adèle, that the situation has become intolerable, that their friendship has to cease, that he must vanish, Victor Hugo replies that it doesn't matter and asks him to keep up the publicity efforts.[14] It is only when Sainte-Beuve declares he can't possibly go on like this any longer that Hugo avenges himself by forbidding Adèle to leave the house, and that he considers himself authorized to cheat on her until her dying day. Meanwhile Hugo speaks only of forgiveness, of goodness, comparing his work to the Alps. He finds himself good, indulgent, without ill intentions. Evidently no one can believe that Victor Hugo was a sane practical joker; he believed himself really good — and perhaps he would have been good if his vanity and literary egotism had not blinded him. But vanity and literature perverted him. He did not realize what he was doing. He never realized what he was doing. He did not know how to do anything except consolidate his glory, slake his thirst for success.

About Adèle Victor Hugo wrote: *"Je l'aime, je suis prêt à tout lui sacrifier, il n'y a pas de dévouement dont je ne sois capable pour elle."*[15] And it is for her that he wants to become famous. Later, in the same fashion, he will believe that in the pursuit of glory he is sacrificing himself, first for Juliette Drouet, then for Madame Biard and finally, in old age, for the servants of Guernsey.

Sophie Hugo did not like Adèle. A true daughter of Corneille, she declaimed to herself: *"À des partis*

plus hauts ce beau fils doit prétendre."[16] She nevertheless
failed to prevent Hugo from marrying Adèle and
making her miserable.

Yet if Victor Hugo had not a shred of passion and
his letters were merely eloquent, Adèle Hugo was too
discriminating a woman, endowed with a poetic sen-
sibility much greater than her husband's (which
wasn't difficult). For example, when Victor Hugo
was writing poems during their courtship (around
1820) — delighted that love was inspiring him with
new literary and lyrical themes — Adèle wrote him
these marvelous, highly expressive words; for, living
authentically in the moment — something that never
happened to Victor Hugo for even a single instant in
his life — instead of speculating on modes of expression, she simply expressed something:

*"Si tu savais combien tu m'as coûté de chagrins, de nuits
blanches . . . tu vas croire que j'ai perdu la tête. . . . c'est
un peu vrai. . . . je ne veux plus être raisonnable. Il faut
s'étourdir et tomber dans un précipice."*[17]

And this wrenching, childlike cry, worthy of Cocteau's *enfants terribles: "Tu ne sais pas, mon cher Victor, à
quel point une femme peut aimer."*[18]

The pure and inner cry of the heart suffices, I
think, to convince you of the penetrating force of
unadorned expression of the unembellished contents
of a soul. Needless to say, we would not exchange the
whole of Victor Hugo's works for these simple, elementary phrases, of which Hugo would only have
made a thick rhetorical gravy. Today men of letters
are seeking to learn the craft by which to forget their
craft: the craft by which to return to the living spring

of emotions, to emancipate themselves from Hugolian eloquence. But Hugolian eloquence, that treasury of mediocrity, that prodigy of mediocrity, that grandiose sum of commonplaces, is a hard obstacle to surmount — so that one might say poetry is more or less realized to the extent that it frees itself from Victor Hugo and triumphs over him; to the extent one understands that poetry resides not in opulent expression but in the naked word, which acquires a new bloom, a new harmony.

Victor Hugo could understand neither this poetry nor his wife's soul. He belittled her.

And he left her for Mlle. Forville and other actresses. Later, for Juliette Drouet. The brokenhearted Adèle allows herself to be consoled by Sainte-Beuve. To punish her, Victor Hugo falls in love with Juliette Drouet. Such was the logic of Victor Hugo's whole life.

"Oh! n'insultez jamais une femme qui tombe!"[19] said Victor Hugo indelicately. He never forgave his wife, or anyone else either, but Adèle will forgive him and tolerate his liaison with Juliette. Adèle understood that because she had aged, her brilliant and eternally young husband needed someone to revive his talent, needed to change his muse.

Grateful for the chance to do whatever he pleases at no risk, Victor Hugo writes to a friend that he is no longer "innocent," as in the past, that he has now learned how to be "indulgent, which amounts to more than innocence," that the "errors" he has committed are making him "always better, always better," and that Juliette has taught him "what it is to love and to forget."[20]

Upon Adèle, in grateful acknowledgment of her own sacrifice, which he accepts without the slightest qualm of conscience, he bestows this passage:

Toi, sois bénie à qu'aucun fruit ne tente![21]

This selfishness, this capriciousness, this incapacity for sacrifice, Victor Hugo also displays in his political actions. Imperial nobleman, he is a royalist, as everyone knows, at the fall of Napoleon. A republican at the fall of Charles X. An Orleanist during the reign of Louis-Philippe.

But each revolution brings in a little something: a pension from Louis XVIII, the Legion of Honor from Charles X and the peerage from Louis-Philippe. No doubt Victor Hugo believed (like Raymond Escholier, his moronic biographer) as a semiconscious excuse for his cowardice and betrayals, that he was not the troubador of one party but of the whole nation (how brilliant he could be!) and had to give satisfaction by joining each political party in turn, as it came into power. Following the 1832 revolt,[22] Victor Hugo, "this great soul allied to a great talent," found nothing else to say in a letter to Sainte-Beuve but:

"C'est un triste mais un beau sujet de poésie que toutes ces folies trempées de sang!"[23]

— From *Ideea Românească* 1, nos. 2-4 (June-August 1935): 105-16.

ii

MISE EN SCÈNE

"La brisure du coeur le révèle à lui-même." — Léon Daudet,
"Victor Hugo grandi par l'exil et la douleur," Flambeaux[24]

VICTOR HUGO had been away in the Pyrenees since July 1843. He was in the habit of going off on long and frequent escapades with Juliette Drouet.

Rather often they were accompanied by Célestin Nanteuil, an unusual sort of man: An admirer of Victor Hugo, he had joined his *cénacle*, organized the first performances of sundry romantic dramas, rescuing them from total disaster, signed laudatory articles on Victor Hugo written by none other than Victor Hugo himself, and posed as Juliette Drouet's husband to spare the poet certain embarrassing situations.

On this occasion Célestin Nanteuil escorted the two lovers only as far as the banks of the Garonne, which they crossed together in loving bliss. They were traveling under the name of M. and Mme. Georget. Victor Hugo had induced Juliette to take this trip by saying, more or less in verse, that they both had to break their ties with the city, flee mad and melancholy Paris, seek out far from hates and envies a little cottage with flowers all around, a bit of silence, some blue sky, the songs of birds. They would go there together, in love again, always in love. For this is precisely what the wave says to the shores, the star to the clouds, the wind to the mountains:

"Be in love!"

Obedient to these Hugolian utterances, the mountains, the stars, the waves, the winds, the shores were very obliging to Victor Hugo and Juliette Drouet. The mountains became easier to scale, the breezes more refreshing, the waters more still and limpid. In other words, all "nature" fêted the coach that brought to the Pyrenees M. and Mme. Georget, whom "nature," friend of poets of Victor Hugo's stature, had identified. The other travelers, not knowing who M. and Mme. Georget really were, could not understand why the valleys were becoming steeper and the clouds no longer shrouded the sun.

The postilion, who was a fine scholar and a devotee of the new romantic school besides, was telling a Basque priest, who was about to proclaim Saint Peter the author of these marvels, that the cause of this cosmic attentiveness to the coach was to be found entirely in the fact that he had upon his person *Les Rayons et les ombres* ("Sunbeams and Shadows") and *Les Voix intérieures* ("Inner Voices"), which he knew almost by heart, and verses of which he had been reciting mentally during the whole trip. Proud of her legitimate lover, Juliette pressed against him in the corner of the coach — if she was not jostled when the road, occasionally forgetting who was traveling on its surface, failed to skirt large rocks — and said to him:

"My lion! I am your little dove!" (See *Les Contempla-tions* ["Contemplations"]).

When they reached the Pyrenees village where they planned to vacation several weeks, the coachman helped "Georget" get his suitcases down. As the coachman held out his hand, Victor Hugo also extended his, whispering to him with an air of great mystery: "I am Victor Hugo, viscount and peer of France, member of the French Academy, greater than Dante and Chateaubriand." This revelation not-withstanding, the coachman spat with disdain, say-ing: "Go on! You expect me to believe that Victor Hugo's got your idiot mug?"

That greatly irritated Victor Hugo, but once the coach had left, Juliette — right in the middle of the road, among the suitcases — said to him: "Rejoice! An unexpected legend is being created around your name!" It's astonishing what can become a legend. "My lion, I am your little dove!" — and she fell into his arms . . . and they recovered among the suitcases.

For three days Madame and Monsieur Georget lived in a little cottage with flowers at the window and in the garden. Their room smelled of pine needles and raspberries. Outside the window lay the road and the mountains, and behind the house the yard was lost in a boundless forest.

Everything was exactly as Victor Hugo had pre-dicted to Juliette: Everywhere flowers, birds and blue sky must needs burst into speech — for Victor Hugo had decreed this as well. But Juliette did not hear their words. She heard only the voice of Victor Hugo, before whom everything — flowers, birds, sky — listened in petrified silence. "Nature," which speaks to the chosen, did not speak before Victor Hugo, the chosen of the chosen. "Nature," which alone recognizes a man when he conceals his true identity — for "nature" ignores social formalities, and before her one would not be able to change one's name or banish one's person — "nature" no longer had anything to say to Hugo. And it was he who spoke. Words that "nature" will memorialize and declaim all her life — ideas, emotions, revelations, which in turn, good mediator that she is, she will impart to other men. Holding Juliette by the hand, Victor Hugo, on the riverbank, on the chasm's edge, his face raised to the sky, to the clouds, stopped with his gaze the birds in their flight, making them descend and circle him. The very mountains, which had not come to Mohammed, gathered round him.[25] The does with the bears, the sheep with the wolves, the hens with the foxes, the geese with the vultures, all formed a ring round the poet. The flowers craned their stems to see him. And Victor Hugo, his hand in Juliette's hand, spoke, spoke, spoke. He made Juliette repeat his words and again he spoke, spoke: thousands of words, millions of words, till the mountains had stolen back to their places, the does to their retreats, the vultures to their perches, the geese to the farm-yards, and the flowers had returned to their normal height. Still Victor Hugo did not cease speaking to "nature." The cosmos was so charged with Hugoism that if one touched a flower it made a rhyme; if one touched a tree its bark said in a thin, shrill voice (bark's usual tone): "Hugo . . . Hugo . . . the poet

. . . the dreamer . . .''; while the leaves, lacking the critical spirit, recited his verses.

And with all that, Juliette Drouet was not happy. Once, in the raspberry room, profiting from a pause between two words, she interrupted him:

"You said we were coming here for the silence, for the sky, for our romance. Speak less, I beg of you!"

Since the woods and moutains were filled to the brim with Victor Hugo, he refrained from leaving the village for a whole week. The children of the village, who thought his name was M. Georget, asked him for candy. Georget, who felt at home everywhere — for the poet feels that everywhere he is God's guest — went, taking Juliette by the hand, to the gardens of the notary, the mayor, the priest and the maintenance man for the local roads.

"Here comes that gossip Georget again!" said these *misérables*, who did not understand that the Angels of God and God himself were speaking through the lips of M. Georget. The *misérables* left. But lo, the village children came and surrounded Georget. They clambered up his knees, mimicked him behind his back and filled his pockets with large stones while he spoke to them, spoke to them about everything. The children loved everything, he told them. He pointed to the heavens for them, and one heard the heavens cry:

"The poet! The poet!"

He showed the little ones God, who was hiding ("Damn it! He spotted me again! Yes, without any doubt, my blue cloak is too transparent!"). He told them how to think, how to dream, how to seek God.

He taught them the history of the world and its peoples. He told them to be good and to give money to the poor. And then, until nightfall, eyes raised to the heavens, he declaimed for them all the tomes of verse that children ought to understand (his), for they had pure hearts, even if they ran away or fell asleep listening.

There was also time for love and for food. Victor Hugo gorged himself in silence, a lot, a lot and fast. He was too fond of Juliette, too impatient, to wait for her to finish. Juliette was appreciative to a point of these ardent signs of love. Occasionally, however, some of them — the verses, for instance — were unwelcome, despite her great admiration for Hugo. There were times when she might have wished him less talkative, less poetic, more Georget and less Hugo. But a curse hung over Victor Hugo: the curse of being unable to forget he was Victor Hugo. And as he was caressing Juliette, he would whisper poetry in her ear, admirable poetry that her own sighs could not drown out, and if it did not prevent the poet from making love properly (Victor Hugo, just like Napoleon, could do several things at the same time), it made Juliette's love life more difficult and, so to speak, more complex. For after the sublime and intimate moments of love, Victor Hugo would ask her whether she liked his verses and what images had struck her.

The leitmotiv of these *ad hoc* verses was:

"The Angels are watching over us, blessing our love, and when our lips meet the flutter of wings can be heard in the room."

35

These particulars, instead of exciting Juliette's passion, further embarrassed her, for she preferred in such circumstances not to be watched by anyone, particularly the Angels of God. Victor Hugo, on the other hand, always needed to be admired and praised, always had to be versifying.

And when the exasperated Juliette tried to put a stop to his rhythms and trochees, he would betake himself to the fields, to the forest, until he found some fairy or other with hair streaming down over her eyes as she washed her feet (*"Elle était dechaussée"* ["Her Feet Were Bare"]), who, taking fright in her turn at so many trochees and so much untimely eloquence, would flee from the poet just as, they say, one flees from the Devil. Then Victor Hugo would return to Juliette with new verses on his lips, which he would blow to her like kisses.

Nor did Victor Hugo forget Adèle. From each village he wrote her long, fervent letters filled with gratitude and admiration. Long letters filled with eloquence, like everything Victor Hugo wrote, overflowing with spiritual elevation, with poetic and moral beauties — and he wrote them right under Juliette's nose. Concomitantly, that summer, Victor Hugo wrote poems on grandmothers and a niece, poems fraught with descriptions of nature and its apparition to him, the poet, in the midst of the flowers or forests, poems on blind and Homeric poets, and so on and so forth. One thing does not preclude the other — as Victor Hugo well realized. Besides, for great poets like Victor Hugo, other ethical standards can be created.

Towards the beginning of September 1843, he leaves the Spanish Pyrenees. He arrives in Agen on September 4. He spends the night traveling by coach. Juliette admires the effect of the mist in the mountains, while the great poet, fatigued by an excess of inner life, was already sleeping, fists clenched, and (if I'm not mistaken) snoring. Juliette could not sleep. She had tried to rouse Victor Hugo, but he was dead to the world. She had been awake throughout the journey, in the gloom, and transfixed by the darkness, the mist, the silence of the mountains, the shrouded trees, the sensation of a gorge opening up in the night, she was seized by a cosmic dread.

"Victor would compose an ode now. How impressed Victor would be if he were awake. . . ."

But Victor did not stir all night. At dawn, after the coach had stopped in a village and the travelers had alighted to drink the milk of some fat buffalo brought by the peasants, Victor Hugo finally got up. Juliette recounted her feelings during the night; Hugo did not forget them and later passed them along to others as though he had lived them himself.

Around September 7, they are on the island of Oléron. Juliette, indisposed, nervous and beset by presentiments, is enjoying neither the beauty of the countryside and the sea nor the poetry of Victor Hugo — which annoys him inexpressibly. Juliette cannot understand her state of mind either. She wants to cry. She wants to leave. Meanwhile, by the seashore, like a painter before a landscape, Hugo

described and versified. Summoned to explain herself
("What's the meaning of this?"), Juliette replies that
she is sick at heart, that she can't bear the island,
which resembles a huge coffin lying in the sea. Victor
Hugo likes the image, and later, in his *Journal*, he
again records these impressions as his own. But because he does not like tears, which spoil pleasures,
excursions and the beauty of nature, he tells Juliette
to stop being sentimental and emotional. By the time
they leave the island together, their relations are
strained: They aren't speaking, they aren't looking at
each other. But once back on *terra firma* they make up
because Hugo wants to make love.

On September 9 Victor Hugo and Juliette, still traveling as Monsieur and Madame Georget, arrive at
Soubise, near Rochefort. They descend upon an inn.
They have their luggage taken upstairs. Then they go
for a stroll in town and through the marshlands. Everyone recognizes Victor Hugo in Georget. A rumor
spreads throughout the town that the master of the
romantic movement is promenading there. But the
people neither stop him nor speak to him. They gaze
at him with sadness. They shake their heads with an
air of pity. Victor Hugo doesn't understand at all.
Furious, he says to Juliette:

"People do not want to recognize me? . . . They
make believe they do not recognize me? . . . No one
comes up to me and says admiringly: 'Monsieur
Georget, aren't you Monsieur Victor Hugo? I admire
you!' . . . These illiterates allow themselves to take
my incognito seriously!"

Exhausted, he returns to the inn with Juliette. He orders beer and sausages. Along with the sausages comes a newspaper dated September 6. He takes a quick glance at it, and on the front page he reads of the death of his daughter Léopoldine, married to Charles Vacquerie for seven months. The two newlyweds, accompanied by an uncle of Vacquerie's and one of his sons, had gone for a boat ride on the Seine, at Villequier. The boat capsized. The two newlyweds were drowned, and their companions with them.

Reading these lines, Victor Hugo forgets to swallow. He dissolves into tears, a morsel of sausage in his mouth. He hands the paper to Juliette. He downs the beer, chews the sausage and gulps it down with an insufficiently masticated crumb of bread. He rises, tears in his eyes, ashen, and in a faint voice whispers to Juliette to pay the bill. He trembles. Juliette tries to soothe him, but she is paler than he. Victor Hugo wears a frightening aspect. His eyes bulge. He raves, he utters a stream of words out of order but in rhyme. He tries to flee. Juliette holds him back. Hugo, beside himself, roaring like a wild beast, repulses her brutally and runs out — where? — hatless, his hair blowing in the wind. Juliette gets up, aided by the innkeeper, and cries out from the threshold:

"Victor, come to your senses. Victor . . . Victor!"

But Victor runs. His eloquence dissipates in the wind.

The wind wafts to Juliette's ears only a few bits of verse:

". . . *mort!* . . . *coquin de sort!* . . ."[26]

And Victor Hugo is heard no more.

Soon the whole of Soubise knows how Victor Hugo has fled like a wounded beast on learning of the death of his daughter and son-in-law. He has vanished, where? If only he doesn't drown himself in the lakes! No, he knows how to swim. If only he doesn't hang himself in the forest! No, he has no rope. If only he doesn't kill himself with a pen-knife! . . .

Juliette, the innkeeper and some of townspeople organize a search party. He has fled at noon. At two o'clock they haven't found him. At four o'clock they haven't found him. At five o'clock they haven't found him. They have searched the valleys, they have combed the riverbanks. Oh, where has despair driven this poor father? It is six o'clock. It is dusk. And Victor Hugo is nowhere in sight. Juliette cries, wrings her hands and beseeches between sobs:

"Great forest, have you not seen my poet? And you, thicket, do you not hide him? And you, waters, has he not come to you, have you not cooled his burning brow?"

"Yes," says a stream, "he came here, his dreadful visage mirrored in my waters, and he said: 'God — the bandit! — has torn her from me!' Not liking the way the echo repeated his words, he went off to trumpet them elsewhere, toward that valley you see over there."

Juliette and the villagers run in that direction:

"Dear blades of grass and flowers of the fields, has not your lover the poet Victor Hugo, peer of France, holder of the Legion of Honor and member of the

French Academy, has not Hugo the dreamer passed this way?"

"Yes," says a lily of the valley. "We have never seen him so distressed. We knew why, for the wind brings us news quickly, and we heard about the catastrophe the same day it happened, September 6. And the stars, who see as far as Paris and are here and there at the same time, the stars too announced the catastrophe of Villequier! We said to Victor Hugo: 'Stay with us, the flowers, so we can succor you. Stay, stay with us in this glade.' By way of answer, he ripped his jacket and knocked his head against imaginary walls. Then he ran toward the forest you see over there."

Juliette and the villagers head for the forest. The trees reach out to show the spot where the poet is to be found. A moment later, Juliette hears moans, scansions, scanned moans and moaned scansions. She advances toward these moans, which grow more and more audible, which become the terrifying roars of a wild beast, a wounded lion. Finally Juliette notices the great grief-stricken poet curled up under a tree, hands on his paunch, concentrating, blind and deaf to the world, holding a stiletto in his hand. Juliette utters a shrill cry:

"You tried to kill yourself? You're wounded?"

The poet turns toward her his noble countenance streaked with tears, distorted with grief, and reveals the stiletto, which was really nothing more than a pen. It would have been a crime to abandon literature and humanity, which were sorely in need of him. He

41

has not committed suicide. He has written some lines of verse. He staggers to his feet and falls into Juliette's arms. They both weep, and through their sobs Juliette distinguishes:

> *Oh! je fus comme fou dans le premier moment.*
> *Hélas et je pleurais toujours amèrement.*[27]

Victor Hugo wipes the tears from his eyes and blows his nose.

"Tell me, Juliette, are those two lines a good start for a poem on grief?"

Finally obliged by the event to interrupt the trip, he leaves Juliette in [Soubise and departs alone for][28] La Rochelle, whence he will catch the coach to Paris. On the way to La Rochelle, he recalls Léopoldine's childhood, part of which she had spent in this vicinity. He would not have wanted to be seen shedding tears, so he just rolled his large round head in his hands.

He was torn, pierced straight through the heart — that swollen and fermented organ which had grown so heavy he struggled to carry it, almost to the point of suffocation. He could not understand how someone can die. How someone so alive, so close, can cease to hear when one is shouting in her ear and fail to cry out when she is being pricked with a needle! Léopoldine had drowned. Oh, that she should lose all her coquettishness, this slender, elegant young girl! He tried to picture her in his mind: dead drunk on water, dilated like a goatskin. It wasn't plausible. No death is plausible. Every death seems an absurd, unlikely fable, with its inevitable "moral": Forever after one stirs no more, one is under the earth, and one stays there.

This feeling of death's implausibility is at the same time allied to an unimaginable certainty that things are irreparable, definitively irreparable, that the past is forever past, that one will carry it in one's heart like a living corpse. Our present is but the living past, the past we bear laboriously, our mirror, our blazing furnace, our sign, our seal. We haven't enough wits to let our dead die. And they all become ghosts who pull us along by the ears for the rest of our lives.

But foremost among all these confused sentiments was an immense compassion for Léopoldine. Now he was reliving her anguish, her suffering, her despair, her own death. And once again he did not believe it. He did not understand death. He told himself death could not be understood, and he did not understand that either.

He rolled his head in his hands. He bit his knuckles. He had no desire to weep. The poor great poet! What had he done to God? And he was alone now with his suffering, the immensity of his suffering. He felt the need to speak to a living being, to ask Juliette whether the ideas that came to him were beautiful, were sufficiently philosophical and sufficiently poetic to make into verses. The sufferings of a genius ought not to remain sterile!

On arriving at La Rochelle, he learns that the coach for Paris will not pass by for a day and a night. He must wait.

He spends all this time in a kind of attic. To calm

his grief or, on the contrary, to excite it (that's his business!) — to purify it, anyhow — during this day and night he writes poems of grief and sends out letters: to V. Pavie, Mlle. Bertin and others. At home, he will show the poems to Adèle, and later, when Juliette returns to Paris, he will read them to her, too.

He was too sad to eat. He made up for it by devouring an immense quantity of paper during those twenty-four hours. The better half of his life and of his heart was dead — what had he done to God? She had been too happy, too young, too virtuous, and that was why God had taken her from him. Such had been the predestination of one of the daughters of the great Victor Hugo. The flowers and butterflies had bowed down too often before one who was like a dove and a swan. God had been jealous. Though Hugo, in titanic rebellion, raised a fist to the heavens, he thought it more dignified, a finer gesture, more poetically unexpected and effective, to resign himself and to receive Evil, too, from the hands of the Lord, blessing Him all the while.

During that day and night he wrote several hundred lines of verse as in a delirium, unconscious of the rare pearls his grief was secreting. His mourning was so deep, gloom had so pervaded him, that he had only enough lucidity left to turn a rhyme neatly and prettily, taking care (of course!) that, for instance, the Alexandrines streaming from his pen, those "great simpletons," be properly "dislocated" in accordance with his poetic art.

There was this grief-stricken hero of humanity,

sitting at his desk with a piece of paper, bottling up his anguish just so the world, culture, poetry, would not be deprived of a single one of his tears, those gems.

A great poet must suffer. Victor Hugo had long been telling himself that some great misfortune must befall him so he would be authorized to write poems of suffering, like Byron, like Lamartine and like Dante or Petrarch before them. And in fact, according to Léon Daudet, the poems he wrote under the sway of grief are purer, freed from his stream of heavy metaphors: Hugo becomes simple, clear. (Here an ill-disposed critic might say, citing not the philosophers but Boileau alone, that emotions cloud and only intelligence is clear. He who is under the sway of grief and a dominant emotion is unclear. Clarity, lucidity, represent a sign of liberation where emotion is concerned. But all that is probably wrong.)

As it was unseemly to broadcast his despair and compose satires against God, Victor Hugo begins by writing the date in capital letters — SEPTEMBER 4, 1843 — and puts a dotted line underneath, to indicate that on this day he was too consumed by grief to write. (Never mind that he had heard the news on September 9, not September 4.) Then, anticipating his subsequent resignation, he writes the poems *Trois ans après* ("Three Years Later"), which he postdates November 10, 1846; *Oh! je fus comme fou dans le premier moment* ("Oh! I was crazed at first"), dated September 4, 1852, and revised a little in Jersey; *Elle avait pris ce pli dans son âge enfantin* ("She had acquired that habit in her childhood"), dated November 1846, with the precise notation *"jour des morts"* ("All Souls' Day"); and *Quand nous habitions tous ensemble* ("When we all lived together"), dated Villequier, 1844. That same day he also writes all the poems dated 1845, 1846, 1853, 1848 and 1847, plus *À Villequier* ("At Villequier"), later modified to strengthen the impression that it had actually been written in 1843, as well as others that he will publish in the part of *Les Contemplations* titled *Aujourd'hui* ("Today").

But at the same time Victor Hugo also wrote several poems on the presentiment of death, poems, as we see, that were retroactive and predated to show that he had a direct line to God — who as it were predicted the future to him — such as *À la mère de l'enfant mort* ("To the Mother of the Dead Child"), predated April 1843, *Épitaphe* ("Epitaph"), predated May 1843, and others.

After having written hundreds of verses, the great poet and philanthropist Victor Hugo gazed at the paper in front of him with red-rimmed eyes.

> *Il est temps que je me repose*
> *Je suis terrassé par le sort.*[29]

And mingled with his sighs: *"repose, ose, rose, morose; sort, port, mort."*

> *Le monde entier semble morose*
> *Depuis que mon enfant est mort.*[30]

He rereads the above two lines and does not like them. He mutters: *"pose, oppose, chose; endort, port, dort.*" He erases them and write the definitive version, in tears:

> *Il est temps que je me repose*
> *Je suis terrassé par le sort*
> *Ne me parlez pas d'autre chose*
> *Que des ténèbres de la mort.*[31]

And another thirty-one quatrains, which he entitles: *Trois ans après*.

He arrives in Paris. He finds Adèle sick with grief. The children are crying. Adèle had written to warn him but without knowing Hugo's exact address, which had changed several times during the trip anyway, so her letter had never reached him. On the table, however, lay still another letter dated September 4, full of flowers, images, sentimental expressions of love and gratitude, sent by Victor Hugo to Adèle during the trip.

Victor Hugo was annoyed: there were his presentiments, invalidated. Inasmuch as Adèle was herself too distraught to console him, Victor Hugo wrote his friends that he was dying of grief. Several harrowing days and weeks went by.

Victor Hugo receives consoling letters from Juliette. Surrounded by his *cénacle* friends, Pétrus Borel, Bouchardy, Mack Keat (Maquet), he tries to forget, and in concert with them establishes that when he meditates, he is a Poet, a Spirit, but when he suffers, he is only a poor man, like all men. Demigods suffer too. These conclusions he passes along to Juliette.

The letters Adèle sends to friends who have tried to console her are once again more genuine, more piercing and obviously more moving than the letters sent by Victor Hugo. Our poet knows only how to speculate, to make a business of his emotion. He never learned how to say or convey it.

Adèle knew how "to say." But lacking literary ambitions, needs, manias and vices, she was not preoccupied by the saying of emotion to the point of cultivating a talent for it. Literary emotion is nothing more than a cheating of emotion. One cannot go into the emotion business, but without emotion one can do business.

Besides, I don't understand how emotions, sorrows, cries, tears could have any "value." They can only be felt, small, human, just as they are, without stars. When one tries to give them stars, one transforms emotion into eloquence, and without becoming a heavenly body it ceases to be pure emotion and becomes altered emotion, tainted meat. If from our human sorrows, our earthworm sorrows, one makes literature, they shed even their earthworm substance. For emotion to rise up, it must pass into poetry unawares, awkwardly, artlessly, without technique and without talent.

Here is a letter from Adèle to a friend:

"Mon pauvre Victor, elle avait prié le jour de sa première communion pour que Dieu nous envoyât des enfants. Dieu a exaucé ses prières. Maintenant, priez, priez afin que je sois réunie aussitôt ma mort, à mes enfants. . . . Mon ami, demandez-lui cela, votre prière sera exaucée aussi, j'en suis

sûre: c'est ce que vous pouvez pour votre malheureuse amie, et c'est tout."[32]

No Hugolian *alas* casts its shadow over this mother's tragedy, no cry diluted in eloquence. It is an inner cry, contained, muffled, without breast-beating, without the theatrical gestures of a hired mourner. The act of living sorrow, of living it fully and deeply, purifies it, spiritualizes it, elevates it toward poetry.

By contrast, the letters of Victor Hugo (who, as E. Biré has established, wrote the sorrowful poems of *Pauca Meae* alternately with the joyful — and undated — ones of *L'Âme en fleur* ["The Soul in Bloom"]) are full of rhetorical artifice:

"Un sanglot ne s'envoie pas dans une lettre."[33]

Here are some characteristic extracts showing his impotence in the face of high tension, his limpness of expression, his lack of resonance, emotion, substance:

"Hélas! . . . quel triste écho . . . [grief becomes theoretical and descriptive] *. . . vous en êtes comme moi aux grandes douleurs de la vie . . . voir la fleur tomber . . .* [an image] *voir mourir son avenir . . .* [reminiscent of the declamations in his plays] *voir son espérance se transformer en désespoir . . .* [here too, just as in his literature, he does not forget to employ the technique of contrasts; and imprecations follow] *Hélas! pourquoi la Providence . . ."*[34]

All these *alases* are meant to fill the void. But his entire body of work is a void; and literary eloquence — a betrayal of emotion.

Adèle has allowed suffering to transcend words.

Victor Hugo acts in such a way that his words take the lead. How expressive is the simple, full phrasing of the mother's letters, where each word contains a state of soul; and how flat is Hugo's letter, bellowing, speculative, prettified by false metaphorical gems and stylistic flourishes. Victor Hugo could have learned the meaning of poetry and authenticity from Adèle, she whose life, whose deeds, whose writings were always pitched an octave above his own. But Victor Hugo was too vain, too superficial, too wanting in taste, to be able to grasp anything. He had lost for good the opportunity to be a poet. The hundred and fifty volumes he left and the eighty-three years he lived furnish abundant proof of this and explain his flabbiness.

For several weeks after Léopoldine's death, Adèle lay ill. She asked to die. She remained mute for days on end. She cradled the tresses of her drowned daughter in her arms.

Victor Hugo tried to read her his new poems, but she didn't want any part of them.

When someone called at the Hugo residence, Victor Hugo would ensconce himself in a chair, his children (Dédé and Toto) on his knees. If it was an admirer, Victor Hugo, eyes reddened, would deepen his frown while embracing his children so as to incarnate the very picture of grief. Yet his gaze remained keen, and inspiration was always graven on his brow. No matter the occasion, no matter the time, Victor Hugo could not and must not stop being Victor Hugo.

"He froze, not uttering a sound," said certain call-

ers. Others sometimes saw him rise from his chair —
he would make his way to his work table and say to
Toto in a faint voice:

"Toto, bring me my pen and some ink."

On seeing the ink, Victor Hugo would dissolve
into tears. He would blacken page after page, and,
his voice punctuated by sighs, read his compositions
to a passing friend and ask if they pleased him. If they
did not, he showed him the door: He could not suffer
those who were unable to respect his godly grief.

He complained that Adèle no longer wished to
hear his poetry — an inexplicable and disgusting attitude now that he was in such great need of consola-
tion:

"All is lost! My daughter is dead, my wife no
longer listens to My poems! Grief has transformed
her into Désiré Nisard!"

Léon Daudet says that this mental torture lasted a
long while and that for many years its echo will per-
sist in stanzas *"ruisselantes de larmes et d'un désespoir au-
delà du désespoir . . ."*[35] Beyond, indeed, and this
beyond is in the literature. This sorrow was a fine,
rich literary lode that must not be left unworked. And
it is true that until then it had been the missing string
in Victor Hugo's lyre. For a great poet needs more
than one string, and he must be complex.

For the time being, Victor Hugo burns with impatience to see Juliette in Paris reading his verses, understanding him. Thus far he has been consoling
himself and recovering his health with beer in the
evening, with the new editions of his works, with
friends from the *cénacle* and above all with his new

political preoccupations. Léopoldine's death was not to prevent him from becoming a minister or allowing himself to be loved by Thérèse Biard (Adèle was too sad, he was weary of Juliette). Besides, he was continuing to write poems in her memory. For Victor Hugo knew how to cheat on three or more women simultaneously without, for all that, cheating on any one of them in particular — and how to defile his dead without, for all that, defiling them.

P.S.: We are aware that Victor Hugo is lately being defended with violence, with legalistic violence. On his behalf the texts of various literary laws are combed to vindicate him. For example: "the intrinsic Value of the word," that is, "the purely lexical interest." But all such attempts to rehabilitate him, however violent, only prove by their very violence the furious impotence of rehabilitation. The huge bluff. Léon-Paul Fargue says, for example, that Victor Hugo is the founder of modern French poetry, a statement that has already appeared in writing several times, though it is true only in a strange way: Hugo constructed a horrible and grotesque edifice. Modern poetry (Baudelaire, Mallarmé, Rimbaud, Verlaine, Valéry, etc.) demolished his edifice, taking from it only the bricks for more elegant temples. The modern poets depend on Victor Hugo only by reaction, so Charles Maurras is probably right in saying that "Hugo represents the decline of French poetry." If Maurras is mistaken when he affirms that modern French poetry is only "the Hugo malady" become chronic, he is right again in regarding Hugo as subjugated by tyranny of words living at large, debauched, bereft of all order, confused, colored. As for what Paul Claudel calls the "westerly wind" in Hugo's poetry and the imaginative force fructified by this "westerly wind," it would be best to beware of analogies and of this "westerly wind," which, moreover, has fructified Paul Claudel himself in such a ridiculous manner.

As for the other defenders, most noteworthy among them M. Édouard Herriot, they employ arguments foreign to the domain of literature and culture, with which we need not concern ourselves.

However, for those who don't understand literary controversies, it is well to recall that anthropological research has yielded findings that confirm our remarks, however indirectly. Notably, it has been established that only Victor Hugo's verbal faculties were overdeveloped, *the others being below average.*

As for the Bordeaux and Thibaudet arguments, and as for the celebration of Europe, that is for another time. They merely signify the fierce will of the French to have their own Goethe, a will all the fiercer for being accompanied by bitter remorse.

— From *Ideea Românească* 1, nos. 2-4
(June-August 1935): 117-31.

LOUIS-PHILIPPE

"On parle beaucoup, à Paris, d'un scandale
déplorable."— La Patrie, July 6, 1845[37]

IN THE weeks following Léopoldine's death, Victor Hugo, weary of the affliction that rules him, takes French leave of an evening to carouse and drink beer with his friends or on other evenings to call assiduously at the Tuileries. His poetic vocation and his political career had to be put in order. A great poet must recover his composure after a cataclysm. A great political figure must master his personal grief to be useful to humanity. The great man must sustain his "sacred spiritual fire," he must himself be the "sacred spiritual fire." And this sacred fire is tended by vestals.

Only Victor Hugo, poor thing, was in need of vestals. Adèle Hugo was still too grieved by Léopoldine's death and had somewhat forsaken the upkeep of the sacred Hugolian fire. Juliette Drouet, herself greatly affected by the recent event and beset by evil omens — and, perhaps, age — no longer had the patience to listen to his long, ardent tirades.

In the winter of 1843 and into 1844, Victor Hugo cultivates the friendship of Louis-Philippe. He pays

him a visit. They charm each other. Louis-Philippe
admired Victor Hugo because without understanding
poetry he had preconceptions about art, and especially because he had the impression that Hugo's flat-
teries were marks of admiration. And in fact Victor
Hugo did admire him, because admiration and exaltation were easy for Hugo (as everyone knows).
His luminous face, something obviously written in his
brilliant, poetic eyes, testified to the happiness of
being in the King's company. Victor Hugo, a
plebeian by birth, felt himself transported to the
heavens, ennobled. Whereas Louis-Philippe, whom
people took for *"une poire,"*[38] a bourgeois with an
umbrella, felt himself King and Majesty in the mirror
of the Hugolian eyes.

This admiration of certain poets, of people like
Hugo, was what the poor king needed to cease cut-
ting a sorry figure in his harrowing struggles with
ministers stronger and prouder than he.

Both Louis-Philippe and Victor Hugo were satisfied. When Victor Hugo chanced to go home or to
Juliette's, he would relate everything the king had
told him: his trip to England, the way he had been
received by the English people, what he had said
about Guizot in front of the Home Secretary, the
witticisms he had heard, etc. When no one listened to
Victor Hugo anymore, he consigned it all to writing
(see *Choses vues, Actes et paroles, Victor Hugo raconte*
["Things Seen," "Deeds and Words," "Victor Hugo
Speaks"]).

Touching disclosures were often made. One evening a saddened, very casually dressed Louis-

Philippe leads the poet to a morning room and, *"lui montrant un grand canapé de tapisserie où sont figurés des perroquets dans des médaillons"*[39] (see *Choses vues*), says to him in a friendly yet pained tone:

"Let's sit in this corner."

And, taking him by the hand — a wheedling gesture that moves Victor Hugo almost to tears, to an awkward, stupid compassion, to an irresistible yearning to laugh, to leap up — he confides to him bitterly:

"Alas, I am misjudged! . . . There is talk of my being a schemer . . . a traitor. . . . You are haughty, Thiers said to me. . . . I replied: I am not. . . . The fact that I allow you to say so proves it."

Then he dispenses more inside information on Guizot. How he misses the late Casimir-Perier, who was such a good minister, such a polite man!

All this Victor Hugo takes down, that posterity may be the posthumous witness of his conversations with Majesty.

These little details and confidences, this king displaying himself almost in his underwear, turn Victor Hugo into a fervent royalist — just as surprising Chateaubriand in the act of brushing his teeth had formerly filled him with a great and lasting admiration for that preromantic poet.

Victor Hugo talked, though not too much, in front of the king. I mean, even, that he spoke extremely little or nearly not at all. Otherwise he would not have forgotten to leave us summaries of his speeches to the king.

Yet this evening, inflamed by the royal confidences, if we can express ourselves thus, equally inflamed by having extracted (more or less specific) promises of a peerage or even, who knows, a cabinet post one day, if he was prudent, he is emboldened so far as to exclaim:

"Sire, God needs Your Majesty."

Then:

"You are the hand of Providence!"—and as a variation, while at the same time asking permission to adjust the pin on the king's white tie: "You are the Man whom Providence has chosen!"

Louis-Philippe, very touched—though he knew better than Victor Hugo the extent to which he was the man of Providence—allowed the poet to keep him company till three in the morning. What they said to each other, I have no idea. It is not recorded anywhere. We have good reason to suspect that they hardly spoke. They played chess two or three times—and Hugo, good courtier that he was, let his partner win. Meantime, Louis-Philippe complained some more and bestowed upon him additional confidences about Mme. de Genlis, the tutor whom he had loved, about some minor satisfactions and a few major ongoing dissatisfactions—yawning more and more, his mouth further and further agape. At one point the king fell asleep in his armchair. Victor Hugo respected this slumber deferentially. Me, I'd have made faces at a dormant King. But Victor Hugo was too sensitive to make faces. He knew that the French Monarchy was symbolized and represented by Louis-Philippe and that it was not to be mocked, not even when it snoozed. And that it must not be betrayed or belittled even during sleep because the sleep of the king is the sleep of the very nation, the sleep regenerating the forces of France. The king sleeps, France sleeps. To respect the king's sleep is to respect the sleep of France and its biological springs. After a while, however, the monarch woke up — he knocked himself against the wooden edge of his armchair — but not France. (France will awaken later, by herself, around 1848.)

Still dazed from sleep, looking right and left, the king said:

"Oh, please forgive me, Monsieur Hugo! I dozed off! Don't think it is because of your conversation . . ."

"Ah, Sire," answered the immense romantic poet, bowing as he spoke, "when a man carries his country on his shoulders, one understands how tired he feels, even sitting still in an armchair. Besides, I had the honor of keeping vigil, Sire, over Your sleep, the sleep of the Motherland."

The king rang for the servants to escort the poet out. The servants had been snoring for quite some time and did not hear. The king, candle in hand, led Victor Hugo down the steps of the Palace and across the courtyard, and opened the door of the Tuileries himself (without awakening the sentry), just to create a historical anecdote. And in fact the anecdote caught on and still pleases today, since Hugo himself, like all his biographers or occasional commentators, cites this illustrious story . . .

. . . But, apart from this courting of Palace favors and his managing at all costs to attend the fashionable dinner parties of the nobility (Adèle, in mourning, does not accompany him), apart from his overripe affair with Juliette and the undisturbed ascent of his literary glory, apart from the many articles about him and sometimes by him, apart from the problems he creates over Sainte-Beuve's nomination to the Academy or the reception of Saint-Marc Girardin, Victor Hugo's life is monotonous. He needed new passions. And since neither gods nor men have ever refused Victor Hugo anything, we will serve him a helping of the passion he demanded . . . in the following chapter.

iv

DRAMAS
AND ILLUMINATIONS

"Le poète s'en va dans les champs."[40] — Les Contemplations

THIS spring Victor Hugo is very distressed. Adèle Hugo is not recovering. She is still so deeply affected by Léopoldine's death that all she can give Victor Hugo is a sort of ethereal and indulgent tenderness. The poems Victor writes, the literary plans he unfolds, Adèle receives with a melancholy and compassionate smile. In the face of this smile, Victor Hugo feels childish and ridiculous.

Juliette too is shriveling. Her heart remains always young, but what can the poet do with the empty youth of a woman's heart? And as if life weren't already sad enough, along comes a new misfortune that will make it even harder for Adèle to be attentive to the poet: her father, Pierre Foucher, dies.

It was springtime. Adèle was in a somber mood. There was no longer anyone at home with whom Victor Hugo might exchange a quiet word. Adèle wrote to a friend, Victor Pavie, that she had had *"une grande abattement de découragement. Mon boulet s'est*

60

alourdi. Il faut lever les yeux, c'est ce que je m'efforce de faire."[41]

And raising her eyes to heaven, she could no longer see Victor Hugo.

In vain Victor Hugo strove to convince her that life must triumph over death; that the birds themselves laugh among the tombstones and that men are like birds; that the grave ought to burst with laughter. Adèle only smiled sweetly at these wisecracks, even when Victor Hugo put them into verse — if they weren't already in verse — from 1835 on, for example (*Les Oiseaux* ["The Birds"]), in anticipation of every contingency.

As for the sacred memory of the deceased, to which Hugo was so committed, he took great pains with it, as is well known: his immense, shattering, official grief was celebrated as early as 1843 in several hundred poems that he postdated to 1851 and after.

One day in April, when the entire firmament was aglow, when all was joy, purity, hope, happiness and goodness, Victor Hugo was taking a stroll on the outskirts of Paris. Everything was brimming with sap, green shoots, life, sound.

"What doth the butterfly bring forth? What hath the cicada wrought?" wondered Victor Hugo.

The whole of nature seemed to be singing a joyous refrain, a song that rose up and became a prayer. It was the baby chicks near the houses that moved him to tears; the rustling spring breeze reading to some invisible person a page from the great epic of creation; the bird conversing with the air; the flower whispering to the sunbeam; it was the warm nests and the blue sky meeting the beautiful earth. And everywhere nothing but color, light — a blinding burst that cried out to God:

"Love! Love! Love!! Love!!" And the sky, like an enormous ear, heard this song.

And Victor Hugo, could he not hear it too? Could he not also partake — he, the humble monitor of the divine voice, the humble admirer of Nature, God's sublime creation — could he not hearken to the solemn exhortation of Living Being?

But the fact of the matter is that Victor Hugo was not alone on his poetic stroll. He was walking with Thérèse Biard.

Who was Thérèse Biard?

Thérèse Biard was the wife of François-Auguste Biard.

Who was François-Auguste Biard?

François-Auguste Biard was a very popular painter. He was born in 1800 — and was consequently two years older than Victor Hugo, born in 1802 (*Quand ce siècle avait deux ans* ["When this century was two years old"]). Thérèse Biard preferred Victor Hugo not only because he was younger but also for his spiritual, moral and intellectual qualities. Victor Hugo was, as we know, very compassionate towards women:

"*Ô, n'insultez jamais une femme qui tombe*" was the remark repeated with relish many times. "Never insult a woman in her fall."

For the rest, each man's glory was of the same quality. François-Auguste Biard, a caricaturist, was esteemed by the great mass of Parisian common people (those insolent petit bourgeois plebeians so coarse and limited from the cradle), while Victor Hugo was esteemed by the semieducated amorphous mass that constituted the romantic public. E. Faguet, in *Propos littéraires* ("Literary Comments") and elsewhere, shows how Hugo, moralist of the commonplace, became the sole guide, the ultimate standard of wisdom and conduct for a public fascinated by precisely this aura, this consecration of platitudes. Platitudes, yes — but platitudes in color!

What was nevertheless Victor Hugo's advantage over François-Auguste Biard?

Biard was a more intelligent man than Victor Hugo. He had traveled a great deal besides, both aboard a training ship as the midshipmen's drawing instructor and on his own — to find portrait subjects, at the North Pole and South America — and he had learned not to overestimate people, customs and scenery. To tell the truth, he wasn't interested in the complete picture, he merely exaggerated and caricatured all things human, as if all things human were not, by virtue of what they are, ready-made caricatures. An interesting and laudable figure, too, this painter who in his travels to every latitude of the entire globe (he was called "the Wandering Jew" of the palette) found nothing sublime and everything perfectly ridiculous, grotesque, coarse — in other words, human.

Personally (though the opinion of one individual

can interest no one today, when the opinion of the majority reigns supreme), I see eye to eye with Biard. As for the decidedly inferior quality of his painting, I say that it doesn't bother me, just as I can no longer be bothered by a world that inevitably furnishes poor material for all humanity's works of art. For example, when he makes fun of such themes as *Sacrifice de la veuve d'un brahmine* ("Brahmin Widow's Sacrifice," painting dated 1838) or *Tribu arabe surprise par le simoun* ("Arab Tribe Caught in a Simoon," 1835) or *Hospitalité sous une tente de Lapons* ("Hospitality under a Laplander's Tent," 1841) and so on, François-Auguste Biard, who laughs at sacrifice, disasters, hospitality, displays a rare moral force of which Victor Hugo was incapable. Thus you see to what point Biard and the great romantic poet were at opposite poles.

As much as Victor Hugo was idealistic, optimistic, grave, solemn in all things (what I love in Victor Hugo, so much that I laugh until I cry, is exactly this solemnity, this serious approach to absolutely everything!), dramatic and righteous — above all righteous and humanitarian, with his faith in human progress, science, communal life, man's divine spark and other such baubles — so much was François-Auguste Biard skeptical and acerbic. For he had grown not only ugly but also very acerbic. He was tall and skinny, a bit bald and skeptical with regard to his wife's ardent impulses. Especially after the Biards' excursion to the North Pole, Thérèse returned — surprising though it may seem — extremely overheated, whereas François-Auguste Biard was more glacial still, ever more

glacial. Since Auguste Biard was a lucid fellow, he
found her sighs of love ridiculous; since he was a
caricaturist, he found his wife's passionate outbursts
exaggerated. For on closer inspection, in each marvelous human sculpture — if one is smart and a caricaturist — one detects a true sense of the ridiculous
and the deformed: hairs, bulges on top of and underneath other bulges — like an Indian statue; sweat on
the brow and in more erotic spots; feet, logs chopped
into five extremities, five wriggling extensions. Auguste Biard obviously suffered more than anyone else
(understandably so) from looking at the world
through his wicked caricaturist's eye. In fact, what at
first had been a game, a spiteful game, became a
disease, a vice from which he could no longer recover. And his bitterness was all the stranger as his
paintings and sketches were cheerful and amusing —
Biard had become by profession and official personality a jolly fellow, an entertainer. He had become a
jester on command. And the more obligatory his jok-
ing, the more his heart soured while his face grew
longer, longer . . .

Yes, the world forges you a personality that in the
long run ties you down, suffocates you, strangles you.
Auguste Biard occasionally tried to do some serious
paintings; the slightest success in this domain was
quite beyond his reach. The world believed that these
too were in jest. Auguste Biard had perhaps em-
barked on an erroneous course (that is, disadvan-
tageous to him) and saw himself obliged to stick to
his path. In this life everything depends on the first
step you take. The first step gives you your entire

future personality. You are not allowed to retrace your steps and set out on a different course. The world needs to confine you once and for all within the bounds of a simple definition, brief and final, which you can never retract. And each individual is obliged to conform to his own definition. Sometimes it pleases him. Sometimes it stifles him. Victor Hugo's self-definition pleased him. As for Auguste Biard, his self-definition stifled him. But that was only natural. The Grotesque is less conducive than the Dantesque, the grave, the solemn and important, to sustaining a good social position and a stout figure.

But in François-Auguste Biard's case, the saddest blow of all was the world's dramatic revenge: His own satiric vision of the world, *hurled back at him*, pursued him into the innermost recesses of his private life. Thérèse Biard, *née* Léonie d'Aunet, young and very blonde besides, could not longer take him seriously. She laughed at him. What was irresistible in our Biard, for instance, were the five hairs that crowned his head and could not be combed for all the world.

In the morning when he combed, Biard howled and swore because the five hairs refused to be tamed, while Thérèse, watching from bed, was seized by a fit of laughter and guffawed heartily into the sheets. How many times had Biard plucked out those five hairs! Which grew right back in the same place like a curse. These five hairs were justly counted among those few rare hairs that remained alive on his head. The rest had long since fallen, like autumn leaves.

How could Victor Hugo — the great, immense, se-

rious and solemn poet, playwright and philosopher —
be compared with that comedian? What a contrast!
Indeed, Victor Hugo was gay, Biard sad; Victor
Hugo was dramatic, Biard was a buffoon; Victor
Hugo had eyes full of fire, passion and genius,
Biard's eyes were melancholy and dull; Victor Hugo
spoke confidently, and a lot, and about everything;
he had an abundance of hair on his head, a lion's
mane, highly lyrical — and though he was not yet
wearing a beard, it was clear he would wear one. And
anyhow, he was majestic, as imposing, as seductive as
if he had had a beard. Whereas Biard, beard or no
beard, would have remained exactly the same.

Victor Hugo, on the other hand, was an extremely
serious man of incontestable moral authority. He,
Victor Hugo, had started life off on the right foot.
From the age of twenty-eight, he was taken for a
genius. Geniuses are extremely serious, highly concentrated, deeply obsessed individuals. They make a
mountain out of a molehill. That's what is called creative energy. But the negative minds — those who
know how to produce a molehill starting out from a
mountain — never achieve success. How should they
be appreciated, those who appreciate nothing? Why
should they not be subjected to derision when they
themselves deride everything? Victor Hugo had that
intensely human capacity to believe in "any issue
brought to my attention" (as he said in *Actes et paroles*): national independence, individual liberty, freedom of conscience, freedom of thought, freedom of
expression, freedom of the press and freedom of
speech, the problem of marriage, women, education

and the child, labor and wage issues, the country's right of deportation, the right to life under a bill to reform the legal code, judicial reform, an expanded jury system, a European army . . . a national army, frontiers . . . abolition of frontiers, monarchy . . . empire . . . republic, the beauty of compelling duty, partitioned isthmuses, any obstacle to any kind of progress, the free circulation of ideas in the universe, all the romantic writers (with certain exceptions determined by him), ministers, peers, viscounts, members of the Academy, the works of Victor Hugo learned by heart in the schools (a bit tiring, but — ahem!), etc.

Listening on that April day as Victor Hugo recited all these marvelous ideals, Thérèse Biard was overwhelmed. How shabby was her husband, that grotesque, that slapstick Auguste (O fateful name!) by comparison with the noble soul of the great romantic poet. She loved him for his altruism, his powerful tenor's voice, the fine things he said about himself with so much modesty but with such clear self-consciousness.

"Il n'est pas d'opinion que le poète n'ait fêtée, et toutes peuvent lui sourire,"[42] said Charles Maurras. Yes! they had all fired his noble soul; his large and generous heart was enflamed by all of them.

They came upon a field in full bloom. They sat down among the flowers, and clearing his throat, reproducing the tones that had conquered both Adèle and Juliette, Victor Hugo began his song to nature. Thérèse was startled and spellbound by the passion with which Victor Hugo addressed the flowers. And with what horror did she recall Auguste's cold, inhuman irony, his jokes. Victor Hugo was reciting so prettily:

"Ô coteaux, ô sillons, souffles, soupirs, haleines!"[43]

. . . when all of a sudden a stone whizzed past the poet's head.

"Ow!" he cried out. Turning around, he saw a horde of children from six to nine years old, all with slingshots, hiding behind some trees about ten meters away; another stone sailed past the poet's pate, and before Victor Hugo could tell what was what, one of the urchins threw out his chest, lifted his head and, stroking his imaginary future Hugolian beard, recited in imitation of the poet:

"Pan! Pan!! Pan!!!"[44]

Victor Hugo, profoundly insulted, lunged at the children in hot pursuit. They scrambled up a tree. Victor Hugo tried to crawl up behind them. But branches, bare feet, pebbles from their pockets and fruit battered his head.

"You don't realize who I am!" howled the poor poet. "I am Victor Hugo, of the French Academy. I have written of you, of your tenderness, dear children — and this is how you repay me, you dirty wretches??"

But the cherubs laughed at him. Victor Hugo tumbled down from the tree accompanied by an explosion of laughter and "fruits."

Impossible to maintain his poetic dignity! The poet is a kind of god. Thérèse Biard, beholding this scene, had the impression that she was viewing a new painting of Auguste Biard — but dynamic this time. Thérèse preferred dynamism.

Victor Hugo, somewhat disagreeably struck by the projectiles and the situation, smiled at Thérèse so as to appear magnanimous. And in fact he did seem magnanimous, with that generous, sweet, suffering martyr's smile of his. He wiped his clothes a bit, readjusted them, took Thérèse by the arm. Thérèse kissed him on the forehead.

"O my noble hero!" she said.

But the merciless brats burst out laughing and shouted from the top of the tree:

"Hey, old man, give her a little smooch — go ahead!"

Victor Hugo turned to them once more, recovering his full authority:

"You have no shame, you young snots!"

But another stone hit him on the nose. So, putting the best face on a bad situation, the great romantic poet, nose tomato-red, turned back to Thérèse:

"Naïve kids!"

But the little angels assailed him with further utterances, here untranscribable, which awakened in the poet and in Thérèse natural carnal appetites; only they were afraid of ill-bred scamps who see into every hiding place. . . .

Soon, quite soon, Thérèse was no longer the poet's mere platonic admirer. Twenty-four hours of love were recounted by Victor Hugo, poetically and at length, in *Le Fête chez Thérèse* ("Holiday at Thérèse's"). This poem is part of *Les Contemplations,* from the cycle *Autrefois* ("In Olden Days," 1830–1843). The poem is dated "April 184-." To all who claim, more or less, to be connoisseurs of French literature, this classic point is familiar: *Autrefois* (1840–1843) is the cycle written before the death of Léopoldine (September 1843). The cycle *Aujourd'hui* (1843–1855) was written after September 1843 — a cycle more funereal than its sunny predecessor, for after Léopoldine's death Hugo declares poetically that he is a new man, that he can no longer rejoice, that his life is split down the middle by a ravine. Actually, *Le Fête chez Thérèse* was written in April 1845, during the same period as the *Aujourd'hui* poems. This is all the more clear from the known fact that he did not meet Thérèse until the spring of 1844, a fact stated unanimously by all the plodding Hugoists and failed biographers of the terrible French poet. Their opinion is perfectly trustworthy. They say so themselves, substantiating their claim with police records (*cf.* A. Asseline) — whose role in these events will be made plain to the Romanian reader further on.

Thérèse liked to organize masked balls at home on her grounds when her husband was away (see *La Fête chez Thérèse*). To these balls came — Victor Hugo says so in verse — pair after pair of lovers disguised as Harlequins, Columbines, Pierrots, Punchinellos, marquises, abbés.

The fun would start on the green lawns, under the garish springtime leaves, in broad daylight:

. . . sur leurs gorges blanches,
Les actrices sentaient errer l'ombre des branches.[45]

and end late at night under a blue moon:

Chacun se dispersa sous les profonds feuillages, . . .
L'amante s'en alla dans l'ombre avec l'amant.[46]

Alone, chancing upon this scene past midnight, François-Auguste Biard, the acerbic killjoy, could find along the lanes bathed in silver and blue by the moon, in the reddish glow of the Chinese lanterns swaying in the trees, nothing but masks, gloves and fans — while hovering in the air and over the empty benches, blending with the odor of face powder, wine, perfume and women, one could also have detected the sonorous souvenir of songs and joyful laughter. . . . The wooden tables under the Chinese lanterns were strewn with overturned glasses, compacts and wine-stained powder puffs.

The guests were scattered among the groves. Biard sat down on a bench, unwelcome, a glove in his hand. The setting did all it could to accept him as a new mask — him, the only unmasked presence in this masked ball. The moon highlighted his long nose.

"My wife's been up to her old tricks!" moaned poor acerbic Auguste while his long face grew longer, longer . . .

As he had a twisted imagination and was, as one critic put it, *"condamné à la plaisanterie forcée à perpétuité,"*[47] it seemed to him that the moon was laughing at him and that his own shadow was sticking its tongue out at him.

From the thickets came sounds of suppressed laughter and meaningful moans.

"Thérèse! . . . Who's she with?" Leaping to his feet, Auguste grabbed a lantern and started rummaging in the bushes.

He found a couple: an upside-down marquise sighing and perspiring through her face powder, her mouth twisted, her flounced skirt up to her shoulders, flailing around in the embrace of a portly Pierrot *sans* trousers (they were dangling from a nearby branch) on whose plump and womanish rump reposed a rose petal.

The glare of the lantern bothered them. The marquise cried out and shielded her eyes with her hand. Auguste Biard averted his flushed face and apologized:

"Excuse me . . . I'm a jealous husband . . ."

The fat Pierrot, all ruddy and gay and still clutching the marquise, laughed in his face and told him to go jump in the lake. Then, without further ado, he went back to his business.

Intimidated, Auguste Biard left. The white arm of a woman sprang out of another bush, flapping gently in the air like a bird coming to rest.

Auguste dared not disturb anyone else. He resolved to wait. He sat down on a bleak, moonlit bench. He tried to concentrate on an idea for his next comic portrait: *Don Pedro II, L'Empereur du Brésil, en lutte avec les chiens* ("Don Pedro II, Emperor of Brazil, Wrestling with the Hounds") . . .

. . . But the lovers had begun to emerge from the groves two by two. Out came an individual disguised as an abbé in purple (who was in fact a bishop, Monsignor S.) and M. Thier's cousin, a lady-in-waiting at Court. Neither of them was wearing a mask now, and Auguste Biard recognized the lady. It occurred to him that he was in fact the host and hence duty-bound to greet these distinguished guests. So he approached them and, tall as he was, bowed reverently to the weary couple in rumpled garments.

"Madame . . ." And he kissed the lady's hand, which was wet from the grass and caked with dirt.

The lady made the introduction: "Monsieur Auguste Biard — Monsignor S."

Monsignor S., the make-believe purple abbé, had forgotten to button his trousers and was obliged to hold them up with one hand while he blessed Auguste Biard with the other. Bending to receive the benediction, Auguste noticed the abbé's drawers underneath the hand that sought to hide the disaster.

Just then, from the end of the path, Thérèse's clear laughter rang out. Biard raised his head. Thérèse's slender silhouette emerged from the shadows and came towards him. She was dressed as a duchess — eighteenth century. She was not alone.

He ran up to her in a jealous fit, raising his fist at her companion. Thérèse halted him at two paces:

"Monsieur Victor Hugo," she said to the man accompanying her, who was disguised as Napoleon I, "meet my husband, Auguste Biard."

A suddenly cowed Auguste Biard let his fist fall. Thérèse was smiling, serene; her eyes shone in the moonlight, and her duchess's costume suited her marvelously. Examining him, she burst out laughing:

"Ah, Auguste, always the joker. With you there's never a dull moment!"

Victor Hugo spoke up:

"Monsieur Biard, allow me to shake your hand. I am fond of jokes. I like caricature too. There is something dramatic about caricature, for it blends the comic and the tragic. All tragedy must include comedy. Laughter and tears must shake hands to realize drama. Drama is truer than tragedy always to the extent that the two extremes are encompassed in that alliance. Homeric laughter must be pitted against the blinding of Oedipus; the Shakespearean jester in turn balances Hamlet. I like the painter in you. You must not think that there is any essential difference between painting and poetry. You express with colors what music says with sounds; what poetry says with images; what sculpture says with shapes; what religion says with ecstasy; what magic says with incantations; what the stars say with light; generals, with troop movements; waves, with their ebb and flow; fire, with flames; the legislator, with the code; stone, with stone; trees, with trees; wind, with wind. And all of us — artists, musicians, poets, revolutionaries, philosophers, scholars, brigands, ministers, monks, officers, seamen, parricides, arsonists, executioners, demimondaines, brokers, booksellers, Spaniards — are striving to consummate humanity's infinite spiritual progress and to commune with the divine."

Auguste Biard was looking very curiously at M. Victor Hugo, recent peer of France, longtime member of the French Academy.

"Monsieur Victor Hugo, allow me to draw your

attention to the fact that you have knotted your tie at the back."

"Thank you, sir," replied the great poet. "Do excuse me for a second"—and he went to fix his tie.

Augustin (*sic*)[48] Biard asked Thérèse, who was standing there with demurely lowered eye:

"Where were you with Victor Hugo? What have you two been doing together?"

Thérèse raised her face to him. Her eyes were moist. Filled with rapture, she held her clenched hands out to Biard and said:

"Don't scold me, Auguste. He said such beautiful things to me! . . ."

The conversations between Thérèse Biard and Victor Hugo lasted for quite a long time, until the day when they were caught *in flagrante ðelicto* holding a "criminal conversation." *

Victor and Thérèse had rented a small apartment on Saint-Roch road, a nest for their ardent, passionate, romantic love. (*"Amour! Amour! Les nids ont chauð."*[49])

They met there frequently to seek shelter from the wicked world, which does not willingly permit the communion of two souls.

Their room was draped in red. The couches, the armchairs and the sofa were red. Red curtains. Victor Hugo had a lot of taste, you see.

---

* Such was the terminology used in 1845 for adultery *in flagrante ðelicto,* for which the penalty was arrest and imprisonment of the guilty parties.—E.I.

In the corner was a bookcase loaded with a hundred or so volumes. The poet's *oeuvre*, the complete set (such as it was in 1845). Several empty shelves were waiting to be filled with the volumes that would come — and did they come — from Victor Hugo. For Victor Hugo, creator of a new cosmos, was competing with God, as Auguste Vacquerie said:

> *Il va sortir de vous un livre ce mois-ci.*
> *Une nature encore dans votre tête est née,*
> *Et le printemps aura son jumeau cette année,*
> *Ici-bas et là-haut, vous serez deux seigneurs.*
> . . . .
> *Vous faites votre livre et Dieu fait son printemps*
> *Et par ce duel d'églogue, imité du vieux temps*
> *Nous pourrons comparer un Univers à l'autre.*[50]

Victor Hugo was wearing longjohns. We discover him in this costume pacing round the sofa, on which languished the fair Thérèse, naked. He was reciting poems to her. He was delivering one of those passionate discourses that always primed him (before) or relaxed him (after). Victor Hugo, who had no equal except among the great, was emulating the Greeks who held forth mightily under the walls of Troy before beginning the battle. Through Hugo's discourse rolled sparkling clouds of silver, the zenith, the constellations, starry hydras, the effluvia of the abysses, diamond celestial bodies . . .

It was July. The lovers' window gave onto a garden. Victor Hugo pointed to the sun, which was blonde like Thérèse; to the flowers, which had her perfume; to the leaves and other decorative, poetic and romantic elements that contributed to love's exaltation:

> *L'infini tout entier d'extase se soulève*
> *Et, pendant ce temps-là, Satan l'envieux, rêve. . . .*[51]

— said Victor Hugo, pointing to the window and turning his sweet smiling face towards Thérèse. The immaculate whiteness of the poet's underwear gave him an angelic air.

But Thérèse, violently jolted out of her amorous reverie, gave a frightful cry and turned away from the window, hiding her face in her hands:

"Satan!! Satan!!"

Victor Hugo, highly disconcerted, took a look. A head had appeared at the window. It was a long, withered face with a disproportionately large nose under a top hat, and wearing a very envious look indeed. It was not Satan. It was François-Auguste Biard, as always the indiscreet husband and killjoy. The long face snickered in an utterly disrespectful and inappropriate manner and then, moving its lips in a sneer, said to another top-hatted visage that had just popped into view:

"Look! Are they or are they not caught in the act?"

Then, in a diabolical tone, to the lyrical lovers: "I've got you, my little turtledoves! My sweet cherubs! My poets!"

And with astonishing ease, he swung himself through the window using just one hand. The other gentleman, fatter and stockier, followed with some difficulty.

"Madame, you are in my clutches!" said the husband, making for Thérèse with a great stride.

Too great a stride. Arriving at the sofa where Thérèse lay, he tripped and grabbed her hip in his fall. He got up just in time to meet one of her fists with his nose — for she was merciless with anyone who overstepped his bounds.

"Satan!" she yelled again, and, by way of clarification, she spat in his face.

"Behave yourself, Thérèse! Behave!" said the embarrassed Victor Hugo.

But Thérèse, lavishing a full view of herself on the envious Auguste, leapt from the bed naked, flew towards the other gentleman, who was quite flushed and overwhelmed, and asked:

"Who are you, sir, and what do you want? You must be crazy to get mixed up in my husband's wicked jokes!"

"He isn't crazy, madame, he's not crazy. He is Commissioner M. (See Alfred Asseline, *Victor Hugo intime* ["The Private Victor Hugo"], the police chief of the Place Vendôme.")

Then, to the commissioner, for such indeed he was:

"Draw up the *in flagrante delicto* report at once, please, and arrest them!" said Auguste Biard, steaming with rage.

Thérèse Biard blanched and, of course, fainted on the sofa.

"But," stammered the police chief of the Place Vendôme, who was searching right and left, "the criminal conversation *in flagrante delicto* requires two parties. . . ."

Auguste Biard looked all around. He howled with rage: The lover had vanished.

"The wretch! Where is the wretch!!"

The police commissioner and the husband pried into every corner. They soon found him. Victor Hugo was under the bed.

"Here he is! The scoundrel!"

Victor Hugo was obliged to stick his head out from under the bed. Crawling out on all fours and standing up, he said:

"I came here, Monsieur Biard, to meditate with your wife upon my new novel, *Les Misérables*, which I've just begun, as you must be aware."

"Ah, really? Well, well! So this is where you write! Right here!" Auguste punctuated each syllable with sarcasm. "And what were you looking for under the bed?"

"My garters, Monsieur Biard, and my trousers," said the great poet piteously.

"Your trousers — here they are on this chair, on top of your garters! Get into your trousers, if you think it can still do you any good! . . . As for you," said Biard to Thérèse, who was pretending to be in a dead faint, "there, madame, take that!" And he gave her a good smack on the ass.

"Ow! You cad!" cried Thérèse, sorely offended. Victor Hugo tried to intervene:

"Oh! n'insultez jamais une femme qui tombe!"

But Auguste Biard, under the influence of envy,

had as never before a diabolical flair and a lightning retort to any remark:

"You, Monsieur Victor Hugo, put your pants on and shut up!"

The police commissioner gaped in amazement.

"Monsieur Victor Hugo? He . . . he's Monsieur Victor Hugo? Well, well!"

Then, to Auguste:

"He is a poet, sir!"

Then, raising his head and drawing himself up to his full height, he began declaiming:

"Ô lac! l'année à peine a fini sa carrière!"[52]

In the midst of dressing, Victor Hugo, suspenders in hand, burst out in disgust:

"I believe you are reciting Lamartine!"

(Thérèse begged the gentlemen to turn their backs so she could get dressed. She was "petite, roundish, just right for a bit of love." And she was very white.)

With Thérèse out of sight, the police commissioner made a strenuous effort to concentrate and exclaimed, suddenly illuminated:

"Ah, ah! I know:

"Ce sont les Djinns qui passent!"[53]

But Auguste Biard was fuming with rage:

"Commissioner, I insist that you arrest them! They have been caught in the act! Arrest them! This is no romantic literary salon, this is criminal conversation *in flagrante delicto!*"

The police commissioner woke up, sighed. He had to do his duty. Biard would not be moved.

Victor Hugo, now fully dressed even to his top hat, had recovered all his dignity:

"This is illegal entry into private property, my dear commissioner! . . . The angels were keeping watch over our embraces: whatever possessed you to rout those dear spirits? Did you not hear upon your arrival the frightened fluttering of wings?"

"Yes, indeed! Yes, indeed!" reiterated the police commissioner, all flushed and bathed in sweat. "I did, I did indeed! But what can I do, Monsieur Hugo?"

"Commissioner," Biard interrupted in a fit of impatience, "don't let yourself be intimidated. The lady has just finished dressing. The gentleman has put on his top hat. Order them to follow you to the police station!"

Victor Hugo turned lampoons and satirical verses over in his head. Auguste Biard laughed nervously in staccato bursts.

The police commissioner, with as much dignity as he could muster while hemming and hawing, finally mumbled:

"Follow me, in the name of the law!"

"Victor Hugo!" sobbed the poor Thérèse, lovely as Manon, and threw herself on the poet's chest. Victor Hugo shook himself and brushed her aside.

Auguste Biard thrust her into the arms of the police commissioner and said to Hugo:

"Come on, right now, you two! Come along, you! If you please!"

But Victor Hugo said priggishly:

"No. Not me, I will not go with you. I cannot be

arrested, commissioner, I am Monsieur Victor Hugo of the French Academy, Peer of France. As such, I am exempt from prosecution!!"

"What about me! What about me!!" wept Thérèse, not fully aware of what she was saying.

Auguste Biard turned bright purple, yellow and green while the police commissioner laughed convulsively.

"He's quite right! He cannot be prosecuted! He's a peer! I cannot arrest him!"

"Arrest him! Arrest him!" foamed Biard.

"I can only arrest the lady," said the commissioner. "She's not a peer!"

But Thérèse resisted furiously:

"I don't want to go to jail! I don't want to go to jail!"

Hugo, wishing to calm her, took her hand, cupped her chin and said softly:

> *Ô noble femme,*
> *Dans ce vil séjour,*
> *Garde l'amour*
> *Si tu veux garder âme!*
> *Conserve en ton coeur, sans rien craindre,*
> *Dusses-tu pleurer et souffrir,*
> *La flamme qui ne peut s'éteindre*
> *Et la fleur qui ne peut mourir!*[54]

And since she wouldn't stop crying:

> *Comme l'aube tu me charmes, —*
> *Ta bouche et tes yeux chéris*
> *Ont, quand tu pleures, ses larmes, —*
> *Et tes perles quand tu souris! . . .*[55]

Dragging Thérèse by main force, the police commissioner dried his tears and said with a sigh:

"How beautiful to be a poet! Why have I not a son so I could make an artist of him?" Then he carted Thérèse off like a package.

Auguste, yellow as a quince, wheeled round in the doorway and said to Victor Hugo with a sinister hiss:

"Poet, you won't be an exempt peer for long! You won't get away! I'm going to have a word with Chancellor Pasquier, and you'll be judged by your own peers! I swear that you'll lose your peerage!" And he slammed the door.

Victor Hugo closed his eyes.

Later on, under the watchful gaze of several neighbors, Victor Hugo left alone. He owed his wretched freedom to the fact of having invoked parliamentary immunity.

But he didn't feel at all lighthearted. The whole thing would be made public. There was no way to appease this Biard. There would be scandal in the Chamber. He would be brought to justice before the Chamber of Peers. How shameful! He probably wouldn't go to prison: Louis-Philippe would at least prevent that. But his political future was in jeopardy. Pasquier, president of the Chamber of Peers, strongly disapproved of him. He would be stripped of his peerage. Now he would never be appointed minister. Saint-Marc Girardin, whom he had tried to ridicule when he received him into the French Academy, would enjoy a hearty laugh at his expense. Nisard would exult. Saint-Beuve would rejoice and wax ironical. Victor Pavie would reprove him and pity Adèle. What would his admirers say — especially Auguste Vacquerie and Célestin Nanteuil? What would the pure and severe Lamartine say? What would be said at Court? And above all what would Juliette do? The tabloids would not keep quiet, and since she followed every detail of his career, she would get all the particulars immediately. How could Juliette not find out? How to hide? How to remain pure? How to extricate himself? No one could help him through this painful ordeal. No one except Adèle. Adèle! Her name reawakened his hopes. Only his wife could save him: suppress the danger and hush up the whole matter!

Victor Hugo walked for hours on end that day without recovering his peace of mind. He was not thinking of himself, he reflected, but of all that remained to him to accomplish for the people: so many rights to defend, so many injustices to redress, so many suppressed liberties to reclaim!

For the sake of the ideals that obsessed him, for the sake of the great causes that needed him, he ought to have made a sacrifice. He should have been content with the conjugal friendship of his wife, Adèle, and with the almost conjugal love of his legitimate mistress, Juliette, authorized by Adèle.

Yes. Juliette was close to forty, Thérèse twenty-four. But Juliette was still beautiful, with her Greek profile, her fair face, her raven hair, her deep eyes, her aristocratic bearing — just as Théophile Gautier described her — and Victor Hugo liked that description. It was just about the time when he left the Saint-

Roch road every evening to present himself at Juliette's and read her some new verses and a chapter of prose. He doesn't go there anymore. Perhaps she has already heard. She would guess anyhow from the look on his face. Oh, he had so many enemies, the poor man! And how spiteful the newspapers were! Ah, freedom of the press is a fine thing, but not when it assaults the moral freedom reserved to geniuses! Here was a case in which this freedom must be restricted!

He arrives home late at night. The servant who opens the door for him is frightened by the torn, anguished expression on the great poet's face. He rebukes her. He mounts the stairs. He bursts into Adèle's room to find her reading by lamplight some letters of bygone days — "to my fiancée." Adèle is very surprised, for it has been a long time since Victor Hugo has entered her room. She stares at him, worried.

"What's happened, Victor?" she asks as she rises, quite taken aback and frightened.

Victor Hugo removes his overcoat and his top hat and, pale and haggard, throws himself at her feet:

"Oh! sois bénie à jamais toi, qu'aucun fruit ne tente!"[56]

Adèle remarks indulgently that this is an old line, that she has heard it already, and that she is flattered by the homage but on the whole would prefer that he spare her such attitudes, get up and tell her calmly what happened. Her father, Pierre Foucher, has also died recently, and in her nervous state she is little disposed to such dramatic gestures.

Victor Hugo rises. Adèle makes him sit beside her on the bed. She caresses his brow as she would a child's. She coaxes him with maternal gestures. The poet sobs. Great tears roll from his eyes. He seizes Adèle's hands and kisses them:

"Adèle, I'm a wretch!" And he tells her the whole story.

Adèle listens ("It is more and more difficult for me to carry my burden, dear Pavie"), swallowing her tears and the sadness that threatens to invade her. Victor Hugo confesses, his head buried in his hands: He is afraid of the consequences; he begs pardon; he fears that Juliette might find out ("She is so jealous"), his political future is in danger, the scandal . . . the scandal!

"Thérèse Biard is young, she is beautiful. The poor woman, how should she sleep at Saint-Lazare among that rabble of women thieves?" asks Adèle. "You should have prevented her arrest by invoking your rank as a peer for her too. How can you stand the thought that you are free now and she in prison? You ought to have intervened this very afternoon."

"There was nothing I could do! . . ."

"We must get her out of there!"

"Adèle, I don't understand," objected Victor Hugo, "how you can be so concerned about Thérèse, a stranger to you, and so little about my fate — me, your husband. Think of me as well! Have a care for me! I'll lose everything if this scandal is not suppressed — my political future, the peerage, Juliette! . . ."

I'll be all you have left! Nowhere near enough for

you! Adèle mused sadly, softly. He is still such a
selfish child, she thought, so immature. And past
forty-three, in not-so-round figures! Heavens, what a
childish man!

An overwhelming pity seized her at the idea that
Victor too would one day end by growing old, aging.
How much longer could he remain an adolescent?

With gentle irony she told him:

"You haven't changed much since you were ten
years old and Soumet° called you 'the sublime
child.'"

In the midst of his tears, Victor Hugo rose up to
digress:

"Adèle, would you please forget that remark and
stop broadcasting it. You know very well, as I have
declared and written time and again, that it was Chateaubriand who made that historical pronouncement
about me! [57] For certain reasons of literary strategy,
no one must believe otherwise."°

And he started to cry again.

This new worry accentuated Adèle's sad, maternal,
indulgent smile.

"And Juliette! What a terrible disappointment for
her!" she added. Without replying, Victor sobbed
harder. His shoulders trembled. The hair on his head
shook as he howled.

° Soumet is the unknown poet of an unknown epic, *La Divine Epopée*
("The Divine Epic"). — E.I.

° It was Soumet, not Chateaubriand, who made the "historic pronouncement," as everyone knows, and as has been conclusively proven
several times, recently by I. C. Le Dantec in *Le Revue des Deux Mondes*
("Review of the Two Worlds"), June 1, 1934. — E.I.

A few minutes later, Victor Hugo, pale with anguish, covered Adèle's hands with kisses and stammered between sobs:

"You, you alone can save us all! Go to Auguste Biard, convince him, soften him up! Plead with Pasquier at the palace! And let's conceal everything from Juliette!"

"That's difficult, for she reads all the newspapers and follows everything written about you. And the newspapers won't be silent. There's only one thing for you to do: flee with her to the country. Tell her that I'll send her all the newspapers myself. And I'll be careful to cut out all the articles and news items about the scandal."

"But . . . the peerage, the palace, . . ." muttered the great poet.

"Victor, just go. I'll take charge of everything else." ("It is more and more difficult for me to carry my burden, dear Pavie," she said to herself, mentally repeating the sentence from her letter.)

"Oh, you are an angel! An angel!" cried Victor Hugo. "A veritable celestial angel! I see the wings at your shoulders. . . . I see the spiritual light in your eyes. . . . I want to improvise for you now, on the spot, the most beautiful poem . . ."

"Oh, no!" said Adèle. "I'm tired!"

Victor plummeted to his knees again.

"Forgive me, forgive me, Adèle!"

"There's only one thing I would never forgive you," warned Adèle, overcome by a profound and voluptuous sense of pain. "I'd never forgive you for being unhappy!"

"Bless you!"

"Go on, Victor, go to bed. We're both tired," said Adèle, patting him gently.

"How can you think that I could fall asleep in this feverish state, gripped by fears of scandal, with your sacrifice weighing upon my soul! I'm too upset. I'd better recite you a poem. . . ."

But her cup was full.

"No! No!" answered Adèle sweetly but resolutely.

"Fine! Fiiine!" And the profoundly offended Victor Hugo stomped furiously off to his room.

He put out the light. He hurled himself into bed and collapsed. He fell asleep. Adèle stayed awake all night listening to the sonorous slumber of the great French poet.

Early in the morning, before Hugo woke up, Adèle went out in search of Biard to convince him to drop his charges.

"Elle obtint qu'il renonçât à sa plainte moyennant que sa femme entrerait dans un couvent pendant quelque temps et que le poète partirait faire un séjour à l'étranger,"[58] writes Benoît-Levy in *Sainte-Beuve et Madame Victor Hugo* ("Sainte-Beuve and Madame Victor Hugo"). Other biographers and historians maintain, however, that the matter was not settled quite so easily. For instance, E. Biré, L. Barthou in *Les Amours d'un Poète* ("The Loves of a Poet") and Gustave Simon claim — as was in fact the case — that the husband's complaint went all the way to Pasquier and that if Louis-Philippe and the Duchess of Orleans had not intervened personally, the chancellor would have tried Victor Hugo before the Chamber of Peers. As for

Thérèse Biard, she spent several months imprisoned in Saint-Lazare, and Adèle was hard put to obtain her release (see Edmond Escholier) and hide her in a convent. (To finish with Thérèse Biard, let's note that she got a divorce and that afterwards, under the name Léonie d'Aunet, she wrote a number of moral plays for young ladies at boarding school.)

One newspaper (*Le National,* July 10, 1845) headlined: "Scandalous Affair Raises Grave Constitutional Problem." And another (*La Patrie*) wrote: "There is much talk in Paris of a deplorable scandal. One of our most famous writers was caught in 'criminal conversation' by the husband and the police commissioner. The unfaithful wife was incarcerated, but *l'amant et malheureusement heureux n'aurait dû le triste avantage de conserver sa liberté qu'au titre politique qui rend sa personne inviolable.*"[59] Etc.

Béranger comments with amusement, Sainte-Beuve with spite.

Lamartine writes a friend that *"ces fautes-là s'oublient vite, on se relève même d'un canapé. . . ."*[60]

And in fact, while the huge scandal spreads like wildfire (in newsrooms, in the cafés, in the *cénacles,* in the Chamber of Peers, at Court, people talk of nothing else), Victor and Juliette are enjoying a carefree honeymoon in the country. Juliette reads the newspapers and notices that some articles are missing. "If there'd been anything interesting in those articles, Adèle wouldn't have cut them out, she'd have sent them to you," Victor reassures her.

The romantic poet writes a new work designed "to

eclipse the renown of the others," as Sainte-Beuve puts it.

A happy Juliette writes to a confidante: "You must appreciate that the love I feel for Victor leaves no room for anything else in my life. I want the world to know how devotedly I worship him, the man whom I love more than I love myself." *

All the commotion soon subsides. Juliette and Victor return to Paris. Adèle welcomes them back with love. And Victor Hugo throws himself into political battles.[61]

— From *Ideea Românească* 1–2, nos. 5–10
(September–February 1935–1936): 231–56.

---

* Letter from Juliette Drouet to a confidante, in L. Barthou, *Les Amours d'un poète.* — *E.I.*

EUGÈNE IONESCO AND
VICTOR HUGO

Eugène Ionesco's most "voluminous" writing in Romanian remains practically unknown to this day.[62]
Some sixty pages long, it appeared in *Ideea Românească* ("The Romanian Idea"), nos. 2–4 and
5–10, 1935–1936, under the title *Victor Hugo (Critiques)*. As the first part of a pseudobiography (never
completed, to the best of our knowledge), it tells the
story of the more or less sensational events that took
place during the first forty-four years (1802–1846) of
the French writer's life.

The book was announced in as a work progress in
Facla ("The Torch"),[63] a review published by Ion
Vinea,[64] to which Eugène Ionesco contributed rather
regularly in 1935.

Although we know Eugène Ionesco enjoyed a reputation for being "whimsical" (at best), especially
after the publication of *Non*, the subject chosen by the
young nonconformist critic still surprises us: Why, in
the final analysis, a biography, and furthermore, why
one on Victor Hugo?

Actually, in *La Vie grotesque et tragique de Victor*

Hugo, Eugène Ionesco extended the polemical attitude that informed his review of *La Vie de Mihai Eminescu*[65] ("The Life of Mihai Eminescu"), by G. Călinescu,[66] published in *Azi* ("Today"),[67] no. 3, 1932, in which he took exception, among other objections, to a certain unavoidably "novelistic" approach inherent in the biographical genre; he held that biography, caught in the machinery of researching precise data and an author's significant movements, would become "spiritually" a lie. Therefore, it would fall short as much of the "imagery"—the only road to the essence of a personality—as of objectivity, the rapprochment between biographer and author being the origin of this tendency to "novelize"; finally, the biography would distort the very understanding of a writer by seeing him not as an ineffable source of literature but as a bookish product.

So in *La Vie grotesque et tragique de Victor Hugo*, Eugène Ionesco inverts the procedure of most biographers: he picks an author whose life and work he loathes and perpetrates an "imaginary" pseudo-biography, which instead of being sugary, apologetic, justificatory and gushy is acerbic, burlesque, incriminating, ironic—even sarcastic.

The interest of this work, then, lies precisely in its polemical character, in its ability to overturn historically established facts, in the pitting of the author's passion against his "chosen" author, all of which constitutes a "negative" of biography, a sort of "practical" negation of the spirit and tendencies commonly informing a work of this genre. In truth, "the biography" envisioned and realized by Eugène Ionesco went to the other extreme. And the pleasure in ridiculing and exploding both the genre's criteria and Hugo's glory is too apparent for us to imagine that Eugène Ionesco wanted to give an example of "objectivity." His game mingles the gravity of his objections, his unique vision of literature and of criticism in general, with the sheer pleasure of amusing himself. Hence the originality, if only in Romanian literature, of this work that heralds an extraordinary literary vocation — which, moreover, has met an extraordinary destiny.

The choice of the "hero" may also be considered from several angles indicated by Eugène Ionesco's obsessions and aversions.

To begin with, Ionesco's Victor Hugo is not a "case" but a prototype — the prototype of the author/authority who, having been proclaimed a genius in his own lifetime, an omniscient prophet, tyrannized the literary life of his era, created the myth of the total author and, thanks to the adulation lavished upon him and his inordinate success, invested himself with divine rights as the proprietor of ultimate truth not only in literature but in drama, philosophy, morality, politics, etc.

Inasmuch as the mere idea of absolute authority irritates and angers the author of *Non*, it is easy to understand his reaction, his goal of dethroning the type of the Hugolian author, undermining his authority — and authority in general. Eugène Ionesco tears down the myths, ferrets out the blunders, the fallacies and the transgressions — above all, the transgressions: the Hugolian lies and outrages.

And then, Hugo's literature is exactly the type of literature Eugène Ionesco had always rejected: a literature of insincerity, a literature born of impetuous verbal delirium, invading literary space, stifling ideas and circulating commonplaces, poses, clichés, etc. The proliferation of the Hugolian *oeuvre*, immense and unformed — says Eugène Ionesco, aware that the principle of quantity is one of the keys to success — is due to verbal debauchery, to an elementary lack of critical sense; Eugène Ionesco trains his guns beyond Hugo's work and its progeny, on the consistently exercised literary principle that engendered it. This is why his work is at once a lampoon, a parody and a polemic.

The often hilarious spectacle of Hugo's tribulations amuses the author of *Non* but also makes him tremble in despair. Deeply buried, almost invisible, a certain tragic awareness of his own situation — that of ridiculing what strikes him as patently ridiculous — gnaws at Ionesco's playful casualness. Is sadness a permanent state for the demystifier? Is the act of demystification an emanation of some unbearable but active sadness that carries the mind along paths of exaggeration, of magnification, until ridicule of the subject and the inner tragedy merge in what is called the grotesque? Is there also in this jocular and sarcastic repudiation of a certain type of creativity — admittedly anachronistic — a sign of sterility that the young critic resented, aware that his evolution as rebel and malcontent was consigning him to a new failure, as he himself recognized?

Eugène Ionesco's writings from 1930 to 1940 are

basically a full and varied journal of pathetic failure. Though not devoid of his keen sense of the ridiculous and playful, they run aground on his avowed inability to express himself within esthetically established forms, at least until he discovers the theater. But we shall return to these considerations on another occasion.

In any case, *La Vie de Victor Hugo* is also a work of disrepute, a nonconformist statement, a sequel to *Non,* not just as an expression of a calling to negation but also because of the techniques it employs: The weapons of the critic are wielded by the hand and with the temperament of a writer, an author of fiction. Eugène Ionesco's Victor Hugo is surely one of his first literary characters, a member of the same family as the Professor in *La Leçon* ("The Lesson"), Nicolas d'Eu in *Victimes du devoir* ("Victims of Duty") or the string of authoritarian opportunists in his other plays.

Starting out as a document of the well-known and much-debated literary facts or literary history of the controversial legacy of Victor Hugo's life and work — especially in the context of the literary and aesthetic storms that raged in French literature at the close of the nineteenth century and the beginning of the twentieth — this work ended as fiction, invention: by exaggeration, by distortion, by a deliberate inflation of intentions. Ionesco's polemic against the conservative artistic mentality (which we will follow in many of his plays) had begun. This time the direct confession is on a secondary plane, but it is still here, as it is in all his writing.

The demystification begins from "on high" with a sweeping digression on what Eugène Ionesco calls "the monstrosity" of the great man, the famous man, the genius, in general. These generalizations shift little by little towards the example of Hugo, thus laying the "characterological" foundation from which the epic part of the narration will unfold.

How does "the monstrosity" of genius manifest itself?

In the absence of any metaphysical *frisson,* says Eugène Ionesco, in "abdication with regard to the spirit," with regard to everything "essential." Genius only poses itself the problem of success, it is nothing but the will to be a genius — any hesitation, any doubt in the face of the great problems of life and death, plays no part in its makeup. Its spiritual deficiency and immense conceit are such that genius imposes itself, proliferates, free from any spiritual stricture, and covers the world with the products of its muddled monomania. Spirituality is incompatible with genius, genius being the perfect product of mediocrity. The skills of genius — Hugo's literary skills, for example — invade and overwhelm. But the triumph of genius also stems from the concurrence between its own aspirituality and that of its public. The public, while submitting itself to genius, foists it upon others as an absolute authority; and thus genius becomes representative. Hugo the literary genius, incapable of any spiritual hesitation, unleashes his enormous expressive power, his verbosity; the unrestrained delirium of words streams out over the world.

By this violent rejection, unqualified and eclectic (resorting to diverse arguments), Eugène Ionesco takes clear aim at the cult of genius. He does not distinguish, because he does not want to distinguish, between genius, "great man" (?) and celebrity, thus fostering a persistent confusion that only ceases when we recognize his indictment as simply a passionate rebellion against the cult of authority.

The implications of Eugène Ionesco's diatribe are not to be sought exclusively within the strict confines of literature. Eugène Ionesco's attitude compasses extraliterary meanings inherent in the atmosphere of the years 1935–1936. His digression on "the monstrosity" of genius, avoiding any direct allusion to political phenomena, was no mere whim, no simple exercise of the author's negative demon, but a clear sign of his ancient and eternal phobia about tyranny (of every variety, in every province of life), a deep obsessive reaction against all mythmaking. His phobias about the herd instinct as well as tyranny are "known" sources of the Ionescan nightmare. Anyone familiar with Eugène Ionesco's plays and journals is aware of them today. Therefore, the attention drawn to them in the 1940s was at most a "delayed" recognition.[68]

So what is this Victor Hugo like?

Eugène Ionesco does not allow us to guess by his actions. With hurried and passionate strokes he portrays a prototype, insists on certain traits without letting the reader judge for himself the deeds of the "magnificent bard." It is only later on, after the introductory chapter (entitled "Presentation, or rather Aphorisms") that he narrates the events in the poet's life that proceed to destroy any shadow of doubt for the perplexed reader. Eugène Ionesco's paradoxical, sarcastic tone is frustrating. And if the Hugolian adventures and vicissitudes merely confirm foregone conclusions, that is because Eugène Ionesco is doubly tendentious: first because he "pins down" his victim irrevocably, as we have shown, then because he selects all that is infamous and scandalous in Hugo's life, compounding it with obvious partiality in the reconstruction of particular circumstances. There are delectably comic moments in these staged fictional passages. Hugo's tribulations are described by the same means he employed for the "dossier" on Camil Petrescu [69] in *Non*. A great many of the scenes and dialogues leave the reader with the (for that matter, correct) impression that he could have foreseen the playwright's career. For memorable images and situations from Ionesco's plays intrude upon our vision as we read the pages on Victor Hugo. . . .

Essentially, the false biographer wants to show the stupidity and utter falsity of Hugo's famous maxim (chosen, in fact, as an epigraph for the work): *"Une belle âme et un beau talent poétique sont presque toujours inséparables."* [70]

The ridiculousness of this maxim reflects not only upon its author but also upon the mentality it engendered. Eugène Ionesco's argument penetrates the domain of morality and enters an area devoid of criteria, or rather with a mélange of criteria, for establishing the value of a work.

We are less interested in the anecdotal side of the narrative, which places in evidence all the sins and defects[71] (which were admittedly quite numerous) of Victor Hugo the man. For the key to this work, its value, does not lie in its "contribution" to the interpretation of Hugo's case. So we shall stick more closely to the literary polemic, the description of Victor Hugo the *literary prototype*.

This "tenor of literature," as Eugène Ionesco calls him, is characterized first of all by the ease with which he manufactures "eloquence along the periphery of great grief, independent of the grief and of the major events in life."[72] Victor Hugo "poeticized and spoke of silence with noise, of death with eloquence, of nothingness with plastic images." "The Immense romantic poet," says Eugène Ionesco, "will lose absolutely every chance of living serious experiences — and his sufferings will be . . . false and literary. . . . He dealt the final blow to emotion by undertaking a literary apprenticeship with an eye to minting it. He could no longer express any emotion, any cry, any lament. . . . Thus, instead of concentrating himself, he diluted himself and acquired an external cleverness that made him glib; instead of learning to keep silent, henceforth he could only talk. . . . He will never be his own master. He will be condemned to insensitivity and superficiality, to vanity, to the venal love of glory and applause that will suborn his spiritual values."

Hugo's poetry, poor in ideas, is the product of verbal "debauchery" and "lewdness," an avalanche of phrases and commonplaces, a loquacious frenzy

101

that does not cease (as Eugène Ionesco illustrates with several droll episodes) even in the most intimate and inopportune situations. Primal, instinctive poet "of the spoken word," Victor Hugo is in fact an orator waxing eloquent with an imperturbable lack of lucidity ("Victor Hugo never took the trouble to think"). He will write on anything and everything by virtue of his incomprehensible (to Eugène Ionesco) "right to pretend that his tenor's voice also ordains him philosopher, statesman, reformer and prophet."

Ham, opportunist, emotional speculator, Hugo quickly achieved great popularity, which Eugène Ionesco explains thusly: "Victor Hugo was esteemed by the semieducated amorphous mass that constituted the romantic public. E. Faguet, in *Propos littéraires* and elsewhere, shows how Hugo, moralist of the commonplace, became the sole guide, the ultimate standard of wisdom and conduct for a public fascinated by precisely . . . this consecration of platitudes."

"I don't see why," Eugène Ionesco says sententiously earlier on, "men are so fond of torrents in poetry and intellectual life and do not equally appreciate in poetry, for example, the life force of buffalos."

Elsewhere, in some essays published as early as 1931, Eugène Ionesco accused literature of estrangement from and permanent betrayal of life, in allowing itself to develop a taste for speculating in certain corrupt practices. The insincerity of literature was ascribed not only to the insincerity of authors but also to the very impossibility of "literary" expression "ex-

pressing" an author. Only the journal, a superior
genre, could still save literature from chronic rhetoric. Such ideas testify to a definite impasse, also sug-
gested above, an impasse we sense in the literature of
those decades and in which we decipher some echoes
of André Gide's choices. The work on Victor Hugo
seems to us an extension, a statement of ideas by the
impassioned partisan of the derhetorization of literature.

Within the framework of this same negative picture, Eugène Ionesco shifts his rejection from the
prototype to the admirers, the principal perpetrators
of glory; the disrepute slides off the "genius" onto his
public.

We perceive in this movement the same obsessive
Ionescan reaction. We have already referred the
reader repeatedly to works that "would follow"—the
plays. Some of the fundamental themes of the plays
to come, expressions of the author's obsessions, are
clearly formulated in *La Vie de Victor Hugo*: the verbal
delirium, the invasion of words and commonplaces,
the horror of both aggressive authority and the herd
instinct, the savage resistance to the invasion of
quantity.

Formal literary reasoning might lead us to see everywhere, hence in this work as well, some unknown
"anticipations" of a now celebrated body of works. In
fact we are in the presence of an already formed
human personality doubled back on itself to the point
of exasperation and exploding into the inadequate
forms of comedy, a personality that has rejected and
will always reject the same phenomena wherever it

encounters them — and consequently not only in the domain of literature proper. As for the procedures by which Ionesco rejected what had always seemed odious to him, they are the same; provoking perplexity and denial, they have always seemed unacceptable because they have always contradicted previous conventions and traditional methods. In 1935, as in 1950 at the premiere of *La Cantatrice chauve* ("The Bald Soprano"), Eugène Ionesco seemed clumsy, terrible, unacceptable, extravagant, antiliterary.

Eugène Ionesco specifies that this whole negation of the Hugolian type of literature is done in the name of what he called the literature of sincerity. Here he resumes his arguments in defense of "poetry-as-cry"[73] and journal literature, which he opposes radically to Hugoism.

The opposition is clear and in turn implies a tradition: "Today men of letters are seeking to learn the craft by which to forget their craft: the craft by which to return to the living spring of emotions, to emancipate themselves from Hugolian eloquence. But Hugolian eloquence, that treasury of mediocrity, that prodigy of mediocrity, that grandiose sum of commonplaces, is a hard obstacle to surmount — so that one might say poetry is more or less realized to the extent that it frees itself from Victor Hugo and triumphs over him; to the extent one understands that poetry resides not in opulent expression but in the naked word, which acquires a new bloom, a new harmony. . . . Léon-Paul Fargue says, for example, that Victor Hugo is the founder of modern French poetry, a statement that has already appeared in writing several times, though it is true only in a strange way: Hugo constructed a horrible and grotesque edifice. Modern poetry (Baudelaire, Mallarmé, Rimbaud, Verlaine, Valéry, etc.) demolished his edifice, taking from it only the bricks for more elegant temples. Modern poets depend on Victor Hugo only by reaction."

One could write — these lines suggest as much — a history of French literature or French poetry in the last hundred years by investigating how the major or minor French poets are situated in relation to Hugo's creation. Apart from Eugène Ionesco's categorical opinion (and not only his), the very fact that Hugo's legacy provoked such storms proves that his work is an essential crossroad. From Baudelaire to Valéry, with the surrealists in between, Hugo's work has been admired and detested, sometimes for the same reasons and by the same authors.

In this way, *La Vie grotesque et tragique de Victor Hugo* is a work that continues the Ionescan "program": the de-Hugoization of poetry means its modernization — sincere, antirhetorical. Ionesco's vehemence turns back, as was often the case in those years, to the Romanian scene; Hugoism has, of course, Romanian analogues: "Victor Hugo's talent is of the same poor quality as Arghezi's — verbose, elementary, instinctive." Part and parcel of the equally impassioned objections in *Non* to the poetry of Arghezi, his references to certain directions in Romanian literature cannot be isolated from *La Vie de Victor Hugo*, a monograph on a negative literary "prototype." Eugène Ionesco reveals himself once again as an advocate of cultural criticism with the ambitions of a radical Maiorescu.[74]

The fact that *Victor Hugo* is an unfinished work is of no importance from the viewpoint of Ionesco's "negations." The author said what he had to say, consistent with his phobias, his program and his tendentious positions.

It is likely that this work rather annoyed and shocked his contemporaries (not much can be gathered from reactions in the press at the time): both as an isolated phenomenon — because it defines "something" of the now famous Ionescan literary formula (fatality!) — and as a phenomenon representative of a literary movement as broad and tempestuous as the Romanian literary movement from 1930 to 1940. The whole sum of excesses it comprises is the product of an agitated, radical literary and critical consciousness. The garments of grotesque exaggeration looked better fifteen years later on the author of *La Cantatrice chauve*.

As in the case of *Non,* all Ionesco's arguments and demonstrations, all his disputation, can be disputed in turn.

Can one not speak in literature today — as one could also have done in 1935 — of a "rhetoric of sincerity"? Does not the type of antibiography practiced by Eugène Ionesco in this work become "harmful" too, as we have shown, not only on the ground of a personal antipathy towards the subject but also because it systematically diminishes all the human nobility of a writer? If Eugène Ionesco starts out by ridiculing Hugo's maxim ("a beautiful soul . . .") — reiterating his earlier view (and not only his) that there is no revelatory connection between a writer's life and his work as far as the value of the work is concerned — does not the very manner of conceiving *La Vie grotesque et tragique de Victor Hugo* show precisely . . . the validity of this maxim? If Hugo's petty soul and monstrous egotism generated a worthless, inauthentic body of work, then is not great poetry born precisely because "a beautiful soul and a fine poetic talent are almost always inseparable"? And does Ionesco not by the same token recognize at least the partial truth of biographical criticism?

We have made all of these remarks (which could have been much more plentiful but would have diverted us from the subject) to stress the destiny of a writer born under the sign of controversy, of a challenge that goes so far as to challenge itself. Let us note that this same theme was revived on the stage in *L'Impromptu de l'Alma* "Improvisation, or The Shepherd's Chameleon").

Finally, there is the copiously amusing part of this text, the "fiction," where Eugène Ionesco shapes the biographical facts into an imaginary grotesque. The technique most frequently used is *mise en scène* (the second fragment, moreover, is entitled *"Mise en Scène"*): dialogue and situations, Hugolian reactions strewn with bits of verse (carefully chosen from among the dullest), inflated speeches, parodies of the romantic prose style, a debased romanticism.

There is much caricature here; the episodes are strung together as in a comic strip in a humorous magazine — with funny, sometimes lewd poses and an often heavyhanded humor. The dialogue and literary commentary are rendered in a collage style — where seemingly real retorts are mixed in with truncated quotations and the author's curt, pungent comments. Eugène Ionesco reconstructs Hugolian attitudes and oratory by paraphrasing and fashioning pastiches to caricature the original style, taking it by an avalanche of words towards the technique he will use later on in "absurd" discourse. Admittedly the author is having fun, but the fun is never completely relaxed. Hugolian indiscretion is matched by the indiscreet predilections of one who described in great detail his own tribulations in Bucharest's literary world.

What then, in the final analysis, is this *Vie grotesque et tragique de Victor Hugo*?

A critical essay within the scope of a literary program devoted to a study of literature's deterioration, militating in favor of sincerity and poetry-as-cry? An odd comic novel in which one sees the possibilities of the *mise en scène* and can foresee (!?) the playwright's career? An antibiography or a more sincerely biased model for a biography programmed to be partisan? A work on the morality or immorality of literature, on the morality or immorality of literary glory (we must never forget the presence of the moralist in the works of Eugène Ionesco)? A mere whim? Or perhaps the incompletely expressed ambition of a reformer?

The difficulty of classifying in one genre Ionesco's writings of the 1930s — *Non*, for instance — is conspicuous. They have that open quality of polemical writings which only negation affords — nothing is finished or final in a negation. . . . For in the end Eugène Ionesco does not see, not even in posterity, an absolute chance of correcting values, of giving them their place. He only concedes to posterity the advantage of certain "stiffer" criteria. Beyond that, as he says in a paraphrase of *Non,* "all human judgments are false."

As concerns the reputation of an author, his glory, the image he bequeaths to posterity, we find always in this text the following reflections, with their intense autobiographical coloring.

"Yes, the world forges you a personality that in the long run ties you down, suffocates you, strangles you. . . . In this life everything depends on the first step you take; the first step gives you your entire future personality. You are not allowed to retrace your steps and set out on a different course. The world needs to confine you once and for all within the bounds of a simple definition, brief and final, which you can never retract. And each individual is obliged to conform to his own definition. Sometimes it pleases him. Sometimes it stifles him." Pursuing this thought, Eugène Ionesco concludes with a significant opposition that is even more clearly self-referential. "Geniuses are extremely serious, highly concentrated, deeply obsessed individuals. They make a mountain out of a molehill. This is called creative energy. But the negative minds — those who know how to produce a molehill starting out from a mountain — never achieve success. How should they be appreciated, those who appreciate nothing? Why should they not be subjected to derision when they themselves deride everything?"

Was the author of these strange passages consoling himself for his own destiny? The desire to "start all over again," to which the author has often confessed during all these years, does it not accurately express the impasse, the awareness of the vicissitudes a hypercritical spirit like Ionesco's must endure to find "the way" to its own adequate expression? Brief notations, swift thoughts that betray bitterness, irony or despair, have already been inserted in *Non* as in other writings, while Ionesco pursued for many years his extraordinary literary destiny.

Destiny will at once have invalidated and confirmed these forecasts. Another "first step" was taken, in another literature, fifteen years later. But it was not greeted with applause either. The negative intelligence — "the one that knows how to produce a molehill starting out from a mountain" — was the same and presided over a new beginning in other forms of creativity. Success came afterwards, perhaps just when Eugène Ionesco least expected it. . . . But it came, along with the need for "the brief, simple and final definition" within which "the world needs to confine you." This "simple" definition is: Eugène Ionesco, playwright of the absurd. A previously unknown definition — neither any more true nor any more false than any other definition. Within the schema sketched above, Eugène Ionesco simply did not foresee the success of "the negative intelligence" or the possibility of its becoming a "creative force." Strange, because it is precisely in *La Vie grotesque et*

Postscript

tragique de Victor Hugo that the literature of Eugène Ionesco appears for perhaps the first time.

GELU IONESCU

From *Secoulul 20,* no. 2, 133
(February 1972): 30–38.

Notes

1. "A beautiful soul and a fine poetic talent are almost always inseparable." Passages with reference notes appear in French in Ionesco's original Romanian text. Titles of works, also in French in the original, are translated parenthetically on first appearance. — Y.M.

2. "on one of the highest peaks of the Vosges"; "during a trip from Lunéville to Besançon."

3. Here is the opinion of Adèle Hugo on this point, in *Victor Hugo raconté par un témoin de sa vie* ("Victor Hugo, by a Witness of His Life," Paris, Paul Ollendorf, 1911, p. 173): "She [Hugo's mother] felt the grave responsibility she had assumed by encouraging them [Victor and Eugène] to drop mathematics for literature, and her conscience, as well as her maternal love, was pledged to their success." [The footnoted comments are Dragomir Costineanu's unless otherwise noted. — Y.M.]

4. In Romanian the pun is based on the resemblance between the consonance of the word "ode" (*oda* in Romanian) and the exclamation "Oh, yes!" (*O da!* in Romanian), so that "No. The o-de" and "Yes. The ode" can also be taken to mean: "No. Oh, yes!" and "Yes. Oh, yes!"

5. "I saw them rising in the mist of the ages, / those monuments, hope of a hundred glorious kings."

6. Here is the same episode as told by Adèle Hugo (*op. cit.*, p. 172): "The Toulouse Academy proposed a prize that year [1818] on *Le Rétablissement de la Statue de Henri IV*. This theme

suited Victor, who, disenchanted with the Paris Academy because of his recent failure, was drawn to the Floral Games, where such a fine Silver Lily had been awarded to Eugène. Besides, he could compete there without encroaching upon Eugène; the Floral Games, unlike those stingy academies with only one poetry prize, had seven of them. There were palms enough to crush the brows of both brothers. . . . Victor had an ode all ready, *Les Vierges de Verdun* ('The Virgins of Verdun'), and he submitted it first. As he was about to apply himself to *Le Rétablissement de la statue de Henri IV*, Madame Hugo got a chest cold that was aggravated by the January weather. The contest forgotten, the brothers remained day and night at their mother's bedside. One evening when Madame Hugo was feeling better, she asked Victor whether he had sent in his second ode; he said he had not and that it was too late to think of it, since to arrive in time it would have to be dispatched the next morning. Madame Hugo was deeply chagrined at this impossibility, of which her illness had been the cause, and fell asleep with much sorrow. Victor, seeing his mother's sadness, got busy and, while watching over her that night, wrote the ode that she found on her bed in the morning. . . . *Les Vierges de Verdun* was awarded the Golden Amaranth, and *Le Rétablissement de la statue de Henri IV*, the Golden Lily. Eugène got honors and the glory of having his verses printed in the Floral Games collection. Madame Hugo having recovered, we again spent evenings at Madame Foucher's [Adèle's mother]."

7. "To us, brought up in the love of glory and genius, V. Hugo was a name almost as awe-inspiring as Homer or Virgil."

8. "And I addressed him humbly, tenderly, as Master."

9. Tudor Arghezi (1900-1967), famous Romanian poet, in turn Parnassian, chthonian lyrical and vernacular, mystico-monkish metaphysical and finally social: royalist as court bard of King Carol II and paragon of the new socialist realism.

10. "Who gets drunk on his own words and doesn't take the trouble to think."

Notes

11. "I want to be Chateaubriand or nothing," reads a note by Victor Hugo dated July 10, 1816 (*cf.* Adèle Hugo, *op. cit.*, p. 146).

12. Indeed, here is what Adèle Hugo writes on this same subject (*op. cit.*, p. 176): "Victor was not convinced [of Chateaubriand's admiration]. . . . Out of respect for his mother, one morning he made his way back to rue Saint-Dominique. . . . This time M. de Chateaubriand received him in his room. . . . When Victor entered, M. de Chateaubriand, in shirt sleeves, with a silk kerchief knotted around his head, was seated at a table . . . going over some papers. . . . His manservant . . . brought in a huge tubful of water. M. de Chateaubriand untied his madras and took off his green morocco slippers; Victor was about to leave, but his host held him back; he went on undressing casually, removed his gray flannel pants, his shirt and cotton vest, and got into the tub, where he was washed and rubbed down by his manservant. Once he was dry and dressed again, he brushed his teeth, which were very handsome. . . . Victor left this second interview with a much better impression than from the first. He wrote his ode *Le Génie* for M. de Chateaubriand."

13. The following are Hugo's exact words in a letter to Victor Pavie dated September 17, 1830: "You know that your applause sweetens my success, if success there be."

14. After their quarrel Victor Hugo wrote many tearful letters to Sainte-Beuve, among them the following, dated September 21, 1832, which ended thus: "I still don't require your presence at the performance of *Le Roi s'amuse* ('The King Takes His Amusement'). Rest assured that I shall treat you the same way you would treat me. To do a friend a service is the greatest happiness on earth, greater only than to receive one from him."

15. "I love her, I am ready to sacrifice everything for her, there is no devotion of which I am not capable for her."

16. "To a loftier partner this fine son must aspire."

17. "If only you knew all the suffering, all the sleepless nights I

have had on your account . . . you will think I have lost my mind. . . . there is some truth in that. . . . I no longer wish to be reasonable. It is necessary to lose oneself, to fall into a chasm."

18. "You do not know, my dear Victor, to what point a woman is capable of loving."

19. "Oh! never insult a woman in her fall!"

20. These are the exact words Victor Hugo wrote to Victor Pavie on July 25, 1833: "I have committed more transgressions than ever this year, and I have never been a better person. I am much better now than in my days of *innocence,* which you miss. Before I was innocent; now I am indulgent. That's progress, God knows. At my side is my dear, sweet companion, an angel who also knows this, whom you venerate as I do, who forgives me, who loves me. Love and forgiveness, they are not of man but of God — or woman."

21. "May you, whom no fruit can tempt, be blessed forever!"

22. In June 1832, after the republican insurrection, when Paris was in a state of siege.

23. Victor Hugo to Sainte-Beuve, June 12, 1832. ["How sad but beautiful a subject for poetry, these follies drenched in blood!"]

24. "His heartbreak reveals him to himself." — Léon Daudet, "Victor Hugo, Greater for His Exile and Suffering," *Torches.*

25. An allusion to the proverb: "If the mountain won't come to Mohammed, Mohammed will go to the mountain."

26. ". . . dead! . . . thou rascal fate!"

27. "Oh! I was at first as though insane. / Alas, and e'er wept bitter tears of pain."

28. The bracketed words (considered indispensable for a clear understanding) have been added to the original to fill in an obvious omission probably due to a typographical error.

29. "The time is come for me to rest, / Whom doth harsh fate in anguish steep."

30. "The world entire is darkened o'er / Since mine own child beheld the grave."

31. "The time is come for me to rest, / Whom doth harsh fate in anguish steep; / Be all speech else henceforth represt, / Save of the darkness where we sleep."

32. "My poor Victor, she prayed on the day of her first communion that God would send us children. God answered her prayers. Pray now, pray that upon my death I shall be united with my children again. . . . Dear friend, ask Him for that. Your prayer will be answered too, I'm certain of it. That is what you can do for your unhappy friend — and that is all."

33. "A sob cannot be sent in a letter."

34. The reference is to a letter Victor Hugo wrote to Victor Pavie in November 1844, upon the death of his young daughter, Élisabeth Pavie: "Alas! how sad the echo your heart awakens in mine! We are both, you and I, steeped in life's great sorrow. To see the flower fall, to see the future die, to see hope transformed into despair! Alas! I could not have wished this upon my worst enemies! Oh, that Providence should have visited this anguish upon one of my dearest and best friends."

35. "streaming with tears and despair beyond despair . . ."

36. The original numbering is II, 3, but according to all indications this is in fact Chapter III, as it appears here.

37. "There is much talk in Paris of a deplorable scandal." — *La Patrie* (newspaper), July 6, 1845.

38. A play on *poire,* "pear" or colloquially "sucker." Louis-Philippe was drawn as a pear in a very famous caricature of the period.

39. "pointing to a large sofa with medallioned parrots woven into the upholstery."

40. "The poet betakes himself to the fields." — *Contemplations*

41. "an awful fit of despondency. My ball and chain have grown heavier. One has to raise one's eyes, that's what I am forcing myself to do."

42. "There isn't an opinion the poet hasn't entertained, and they can all smile upon him."

43. "O hills, O furrows, breezes, sighs, winds!"

44. "Bang! Bang!! Bang!!!"

45. ". . . upon their bosoms white, / The actresses felt the trees' shadow alight."

46. "They scattered one and all 'neath the foliage so dense, . . . / Lover with beloved to the shadows did fly."

47. "sentenced to a life term of jokes."

48. Auguste, a popular name for a clown, is here changed to the saint's name.

49. "Love! Love! The nests are warm."

50. "A book this month will come from thee. / Another nature is born in thy mind, / And Springtime this year its twin will find, / Here below, up above, two Lords there will be. . . . / Thou makest thy book, and God His spring / A pastoral duel as of yore men did sing / That each Universe we may to the other compare."

51. "All infinity rises up in ecstasy sublime, / And Satan the envious dreams the whole time. . . ."

52. "O lake! hardly spent is the long span of the year!"

53. "The Djinns are marching by!"

54. "O woman of noble soul, / In this vile place / Your love embrace / To keep your spirit whole. / Hold in your heart, be not afraid, / Though perchance you grieve and cry, / The burning flame that cannot fade / And the flower that ne'er can die."

55. "You charm me like the breaking dawn, / Your mouth and your dear eyes / With teardrops fill whene'er you mourn — / Pearls when your smile doth rise!. . ."

56. "Oh! May you be blessed forever, whom no fruit can tempt!"

57. Here, in fact, are several passages from Adèle's version of the paternity of this "historical pronouncement," to which she devotes an entire chapter, *"Un mot de Chateaubriand"* ("A Word from Chateaubriand") of her book on Hugo (*op. cit.*, p. 175): "M. de Chateaubriand, while chatting with a deputy of the right, M. Agier, spoke to him of the ode [on the death of the Duke of Berry in 1820 — when Victor Hugo was eighteen!] in enthusiastic terms and told him that the author was a *sublime child*. . . . This pronouncement by the great writer was repeated everywhere, and Victor became a true celebrity." According to Adèle, Soumet's first appearance in the literary career of Victor Hugo took the form of a letter of congratulation on his participation in the Toulouse Academy competition (*op. cit.*, p. 172): "Since we received your odes, sir, I hear nothing all around me but talk of your fine talent and the prodigious hopes you bestow upon our literature. If the Academy shares my sentiments, Isaure will not have enough laurels for you and your brother. Your seventeen years awaken nothing but admiration here, unless it be incredulity. For us you are an enigma to which the muses hold the key. I remain, etc., SOUMET." [Clémence Isaure was thought to have founded the Toulouse Academy in the fourteenth century, but that opinion has been refuted by modern research. — Y.M.]

58. "She persuaded him to waive his accusation on condition that his wife enter a convent for a while and that the poet take up temporary residence abroad."

59. "the lover — a happy man, unhappily — owes the distressing advantage of his continued freedom only to the political title which exempts him from prosecution."

60. "such faults are quickly forgotten, and one rises again even from a sofa. . . ."

61. Here ends the publication of this work of Eugène Ionesco's in the review *Ideea Românească* ("The Romanian Idea"); the rest of the text has not (yet) been located.

62. Eugène Ionesco's most voluminous writing is *Non* ("No"), a collection of criticism published in 1934 by Vremea, Bucharest.

63. In its issue of November 30, 1935, *Facla* announced under a tentative title: *Victor Hugo* or *Génie, amour, folie et mort* ("Genius, Love, Folly and Death") or *La Vie solennelle de Victor Hugo* ("The Solemn Life of Victor Hugo"). Then on February 7, 1936, shortly before Eugène Ionesco became its literary reviewer for a year, *Facla* announced *La Vie grotesque et tragique de Victor Hugo*, specifying that three quarters of the total pages in the planned volume would be devoted to the "agony" of Victor Hugo. Finally, the following notice appeared in the issue of *Facla* dated July 9, 1936: "Eugène Ionesco, our contributor, professor of French at Cernavodă . . . is working on *La Vie et la mort de Victor Hugo* ('The Life and Death of Victor Hugo'). If the author of *Les Misérables* were not immortal, the eminent critic could have killed him (?); as it is, the poor Ahasuerus will escape unscathed. . . ." Stopping where it does, *La Vie de Victor Hugo* does not give us the opportunity to ascertain how Eugène Ionesco set the stage for the poet's agony. Might we have arrived at an anticipation of the tragic destinies of some of the characters of his future plays? — G.I.

64. Ion Vinea (1895–1964): Romanian poet, prose writer, translator and journalist.

65. Mihai Eminescu (1850–1889): famous Romanian romantic poet and prose writer.

66. Gheorghe Călinescu (1899–1965): critic, literary historian, poet and prose writer. He wrote many monographs on Mihai Eminescu: *Mihai Eminescu: Studies and Articles*, 1928; *The Life of Mihai Eminescu*, 1932; *The Works of Mihai Eminescu*, 1934; etc.

Notes

67. *Azi* (1932-1938; 1939-1940): progressive weekly review of literature and criticism directed by the writer Zaharia Stancu, to which Eugène Ionesco contributed until about 1935.

68. On the shock experienced by the author during the initial years of the fascist dictatorships, and its echo in his plays, see *Notes et contre-notes* ("Notes and Counternotes"), Gallimard, 1966, pp. 277ff. — G.I.

69. Camil Petrescu (1894-1957): Romanian prose writer, playwright, poet and essayist.

70. From a letter written by Victor Hugo to his fiancée (as specified by Eugène Ionesco). — G.I.

71. Boundless ambition, "limited intelligence," enormous political opportunism, demagoguery, "monstrous egotism," jealousy towards all other literary glory (a basically nonspecific transgression) are not overlooked by Eugène Ionesco. We might quote Thierry Maulnier ("V. Hugo has no trace of humility, irony or self-consciousness") and Éd. Biré, who stresses the French poet's "detestable moral physiognomy." But what seems to irritate Eugène Ionesco most is Hugo's political conformism (see the description of his friendship with Louis-Philippe), and similarly, in his private life, his egotism "motivated" by a false messianic posture. — G.I.

72. Supported by documentation, Eugène Ionesco emphasizes the notorious "redating" practiced by Hugo to establish a direct connection between his sad poems and certain serious or tragic events in his life. — G.I.

73. Here Gelu Ionescu quotes in full Ionesco's definition of "poetry-as-cry," which begins and ends as follows: "Poetry is not lexical expression. . . . poetry has only a spiritual primitiveness." However, we considered it unnecessary to repeat the whole passage, which the reader can easily find by referring to pages 18-20 of the present volume.

74. Titu Maiorescu (1840-1917): philosopher, critic and aesthetician, cultural theorist, "spiritual father" of Romanian literary criticism, defender of modernism.

Chronological Table

EUGÈNE IONESCO
AND ROMANIA

Childhood and first stay in France

1909   Birth of Eugen Ionescu (Romanian spelling) at Slatina, Romania, on November 13, according to the research of Professor Gheorghe Mihai in the Slatina State Archives, as furnished to and published in the review *România Literară* ("Literary Romania"), no. 28, 1969. He is the son of Eugen Ionescu, a lawyer who obtained his degree from the Paris law school, and of Thérèse, of French origin.

1911   Stay in Paris; attends primary school on rue Dupleix.

1921   Stay of two and a half years (with his sister) at La Chapelle-Anthenaise in Mayenne.

1923   Return to Paris.

First literary creation

1923   Writes a historical drama that he will later "translate" into Romanian.

Chronology

Return to Romania and secondary schooling

1924 Eugen Ionescu goes back to Romania and learns Romanian. Attends the Sfântul Sava school in Bucharest.

1928 Passes the baccalaureate at the Craiova lycée.

Literary debut

1928 He debuts as a poet in *Bilete de papagal* ("Parrot Notes"), a daily review famous for its minuscule format and for having launched a new genre consisting of "billets" or "tablets"; it was directed by the poet Tudor Arghezi.

College education

1928–
1933 Takes courses at the Faculty of Arts in Bucharest, preparing for a bachelor's degree in French.

First literary contributions

1928–
1935 Engages in sustained literary activity as a poet and critic, with contributions to several reviews, among them:
— *Vremea* ("The Times"), a political, social and cultural weekly publishing an eclectic selection of literature under the direction of Vladimir Al. Donescu;
— *Azi* ("Today"), a progressive weekly of the new generation, concerned with literature, criticism and art, under the direction of the writer Zaharia Stancu;
— *Viaţa Literară* ("Literary Life"), a moderate monthly directed by the poet G. Murnu;
— *România Literară* ("Literary Romania"), a

weekly of criticism and literary, artistic and cultural information, not aligned with any precise literary trend or orientation, one of the most prestigious reviews of the period, with a high aesthetic level, directed by the noted writer Liviu Rebreanu;

— *Critica* ("Criticism"), a leftist and antifascist weekly directed by the painter Gh. Labin;

— and also *Axa* ("The Axis"), *Floarea de foc* ("The Fire Flower"), *Ideea Românească* ("The Romanian Idea") and *Zodiac.*

Books published

1931 *Elegii pentru fiinte mici* ("Elegies for Minuscule Beings"), a booklet of verse published by Cercul Analelor Române, Craiova.

1932 Second edition of *Elegii* published in Bucharest.

1934 Vremea, in Bucharest, publishes *Nu* ("No"), a volume of protest criticism that provokes a huge scandal in the Romanian literary world because of its destructive, subversive attack, conducted with great verve and sarcasm, on the consecrated values of Romanian literature, as represented by Tudor Arghezi, Ion Barbu, Camil Petrescu, Mircea Eliade. The book receives the Royal Foundations Editions prize, awarded by a jury presided over by the critic and literary theorist Tudor Vianu.

Events in private life

1936 Death of his mother. Marriage to Rodica Burileanu. Works as professor of French at Cernavodà.

Chronology

1937 Works briefly as professor of French at the Sfântul Sava school in Bucharest.

1938 Obtains a scholarship from the French government to prepare in Paris a doctoral dissertation ("The Themes of Sin and Death in French Poetry after Baudelaire").

Last contributions before leaving for Paris

1936– Frequent contributor to:

1938 — *Facla* ("The Torch"), a democratic and anti-royalist weekly agitating for social justice, directed by N. D. Cocea and Ion Vinea;

— *Universul Literar* ("The Literary Universe"), supplement of the newspaper *Universul*;

— *Rampa* ("The Ramp"), a daily sheet on theatrical, musical, literary and artistic topics, directed by the writers Al. Davilla and N. D. Cocea;

— and also *Păreri Libere* ("Free Opinions").

1939 Contributes, from Paris, to *Viaţa Românească* ("Romanian Life"), a prestigious literary and scientific review published monthly, directed by Mihai Ralea, aesthetician and philosopher, and G. Călinescu, critic and literary theorist.

Translator from Romanian

1945 Translates and writes preface to *Urcan Bătrânul* ("Old Urcan"), a novel by Pavel Dan (1907–1937), published by J. Vigneau, Marseille.

1945– Translates the works of Urmuz (1883–1923), a

1949 Romanian poet, precursor of surrealism, the literature of the absurd and antiprose.

Hugoliaд

1968 Writes preface to *Onze Récits* ("Eleven Narratives"), by Ilarie Voronca (1903–1946), Romanian poet of the avant-garde, futurist, dadaist, surrealist, published by Rougerie, Limoges.

First "absurд" play

1948 Writes, in Romanian, the first variant of *La Cantatrice chauve* ("The Bald Soprano"), under the title *Englezeşte fără profesor* ("English without a Teacher").

Translator into Romanian

1964 First publication in Romania of two volumes of plays, by Pentru Literatură Universală, Bucharest.

1970 Two other volumes of plays (including many reprints from the previous two volumes), published by Minerva, Bucharest.

1973 Last translation: *Jeux дe massacre* ("Killing Game"), published by Univers, Bucharest.

Plays performeд in Romania

1964 First performance of an Ionesco play in Romania: *Rhinocéros*, at the Théâtre de Comédie, Bucharest.

1965 Three premiers in Bucharest: *La Cantatrice chauve*, *Les Chaises* ("The Chairs") and *Le Roi se meurt* ("Exit the King").

1968 Two more premieres in Bucharest: *Tueur sans gages* ("The Killer") and *Victimes дu дevoir* ("Victims of Duty").